# Praise for the Authors

*"Who Gets the Farm addresses the most significant challenges impacting the sustainability of family farming in Australia right now. Family farming is in crisis effecting individuals, families and communities. We need to address the issue of farm succession planning, to ensure the sustainability and viability of farming for future generations."*

**Michael Nash,**
**Senior Researcher of Grains Entomology**
**at SARDI & Former Farmer**

*"I can identify with the personal stories shared in Who Gets the Farm. I would have liked to have this book when I was going through my own succession planning process. Nick and Ayesha have taken a complex topic and broken it down into simple steps. I highly recommend this book to other farming families who want to create a succession plan and ensure the future viability of their farming enterprise."*

**Kevin Moloney,**
**Procurement Management**
**at Ridley AgriProducts & Former Dairy Farmer**

*"Our firm regularly helps clients navigate the complex terrain that is succession planning. We've seen how challenging it can be for families and how stressful it can be. We've also seen how essential succession planning is and what happens when a family doesn't have a good plan or has no plan at all. Who Gets the Farm will help a lot of families understand what is involved in the succession planning process."*

**Paul Hansen,**
**Partner & Accountant,**
**MOR Accountants Ballarat**

# Who Gets the Farm?

**GLOBAL**
PUBLISHING
G R O U P

**Global Publishing Group**
Australia • New Zealand • Singapore • America • London

"Must have book for farming families"

# Who Gets the Farm?

## A practical guide to farm succession planning

**Nick Shady & Ayesha Hilton**

DISCLAIMER

All the information, techniques, skills and concepts contained within this publication are of the nature of general comment only and are not in any way recommended as individual advice. The intent is to offer a variety of information to provide a wider range of choices now and in the future, recognising that we all have widely diverse circumstances and viewpoints. Should any reader choose to make use of the information contained herein, this is their decision, and the contributors (and their companies), authors and publishers do not assume any responsibilities whatsoever under any condition or circumstances. It is recommended that the reader obtain their own independent advice.

First Edition 2015

Copyright © 2015 Nicholas Shady and Ayesha Hilton

National Library of Australia
Cataloguing-in-Publication entry:

Creator: Nick Shady and Ayesha Hilton, authors.

Who Gets The Farm? : A Practical Guide to Farm Succession Planning /
Nick Shady & Ayesha Hilton.

1st ed.
ISBN: 9781925288087 (paperback)

Family farms – Finance.
Family farms – Management.
Family-owned business enterprises – Succession.
Family-owned business enterprises – Case studies.

Dewey Number: 630.681

Published by Global Publishing Group
PO Box 517 Mt Evelyn, Victoria 3796 Australia
Email info@GlobalPublishingGroup.com.au

For further information about orders:
Phone: +61 3 9739 4686 or Fax +61 3 8648 6871

# Acknowledgements

In any major undertaking, including writing and publishing a book, there are so many people whose support helps bring a dream into reality.

We are passionate about family farming and have had so much support in our farming journey. We would like to acknowledge Nick's brother, Chris Shady, who allowed us to gracefully and easily transition the family farming business into separate enterprises. This has enabled our family to follow our own dreams and to farm in the way most suited to our lifestyle. Thank you also to Nick's parents, Bill and Yvonne Shady, for their continued support and sharing their love of farming.

We would also like to publicly thank our friends and family for their support. Thank you to Grandpa (Shaun Flanagan) for having adventures with Grace and Spencer while we worked to a tight deadline. Thank you to Ayesha's mum, Judy Kenyon, and step father, Derek High, for their understanding of our vision. Thank you to Ayesha's friends Yvette Knights, Susan Whitelaw and the Stokes family (Angie, Katie, Pat) for their friendship and support over the years.

Our professional services team have provided us with ongoing support in our family farming business and our succession planning process as well as with input into this book. In particular, we wish to thank:

- Paul Hansen and Danny Molloy and their team at MOR Accounting
- Trevor Madden of AJ Gallagher (formerly OAMPS Ballarat)
- Dean Cinque of COS Lawyers
- Ballarat NAB Agribusiness - Duncan Ritchie, Stuart Postlethwaite and their team

Thank you to all those farming families that completed our farm succession planning survey or shared their stories with us. We undertook extensive research for this book and would like to acknowledge the various references we have consulted.

We would not have even dreamt of this book if it wasn't for Darren Stephens and Jackie Tallentrye of the Global Publishing Group. They and their team are an inspiration and have made the process of writing this book easy even during the challenges. Their stable of amazing writers has also been an inspiration and we have formed many lifelong friendships with many of them.

One of the main drivers for writing this book is the mental wellbeing of farming families. There is such a high rate of suicide in rural and regional Australia and we hope that by talking openly about succession planning and other things that cause stress in family farming, we can have a real impact on people's lives.

We proudly support Survivors of Suicide that was founded by Kristy Steenhuis. Kristy, your suffering has given you the motivation to help others who have lost loved ones to suicide. We thank you for all your hard work and will continue to support you in your mission.

During our lives, we have come across so many great teachers and leaders who have changed our lives with their wisdom and knowledge. Ayesha has taken inspiration from many famous role models and teachers, including H.H. the Dalai Lama, Dr De Martini, Oprah Winfrey, Dr Dwayne Dwyer, Richard Branson, Nelson Mandela and Louise Hay.

Thank you to all the other people not listed here who helped us along the way. We feel very blessed to have the love and support of so many amazing people.

Our wish is that this book will help other farming families, so we thank all those who read this book and utilise it for creating and implementing a succession plan that they and their family are happy with.

*With gratitude,*

*Ayesha Hilton & Nick Shady*

*We dedicate this book to all those families working the land to create a better future. Our hope is that this book will serve as an inspiration and a practical guide to ensure that you and your family can remain happily in farming for as long as you wish.*

*We also dedicate this book to Spencer and Grace, who are our inspiration and motivation to create the most amazing life for our family.*

**Ayesha & Nick**

# Disclaimer

We, Ayesha Hilton and Nick Shady, are not succession planners, lawyers or financial planners. We are just two people who are passionate about family farming. We have researched and consolidated the information about succession planning in this book to help guide you on your succession planning journey.

We accept no liability for any loss whatsoever including consequential loss suffered by you arising from information provided in this book. We highly recommend you see a qualified professional before you make any decisions, financial or otherwise.

# Contents

# Foreword

Agriculture in Australia is embedded in our history, traditions, literature and culture. Agriculture has provided us with our sense of identity and community, whilst also being of economic and social significance across our rural and regional landscapes.

Agriculture and its role in our economy arises from the agricultural technologies bought with the first settlers from their homeland in the late 1700's, to 'riding on the sheep's back' in the mid 1800's to dairying in the early 1900's to the mixed enterprise of today. Agriculture has not only brought profit to many, but has sustained rural communities and contributed significantly to our country's economic growth.

As pivotal as agriculture is to our economy, so too is it to our rural ideology. Farmers and their way of life are part of our nation's distinctive character. Farming is portrayed as an idyllic lifestyle punctuated with hard work, innovation, ingenuity and independence. In the past agriculture in Australia was viewed by the agrarian myth and the patrilineal nature of the farming institution, a notion that in some instances continues to pervade our image of agricultural communities and farmers and how they manage their business.

Today, agriculture operates in a highly competitive global market place. Consequently the industry has had to adapt to complex social, legal, political, environmental and economic conditions. As we move towards the future and address the challenges of future food production, there will also be many challenges and opportunities for our agricultural economy, landscape and production systems.

A recent challenge which has been recognised by the industry is that of farm succession planning. The patrilineal or traditional methods of inheritance are no longer deemed as a feasible way to manage the intergenerational transfer of farms and farm assets.

Farm succession planning is the orderly transfer of management, responsibility, ownership and control, over time of the farm business. Farm succession planning is a complex and in some instances a confronting process, but with proper planning it doesn't need to be divisive.

"Who Gets the Farm? A Practical Guide to Farm Succession Planning" is an important book that details how to communicate with your family to minimise disputes and conflict when it comes to Farm Succession Planning. It also demonstrates how important it is to protect the people that matter the most, your family.

The vision of Nick and Ayesha to produce this book is commendable. They have written this book as a way to express their experiences and journey from family farming partner to financial and business independence. They share practical strategies to help everyday farmers get real about succession planning and to motivate them to take action.

What is demonstrated in this book is that with good family communication and the right people to guide the business, a positive farm succession plan can be implemented. A plan where all members of the family can feel that they are valued and, more importantly, the whole family can enjoy what life has given them.

*Dan Tehan*
*Member for Wannon*

# Introduction

Does the mere mention of "succession planning" make you shudder? Have you experienced or heard horror stories of succession planning gone bad? Are you in a situation in your farming business where you need to really think about succession planning?

Succession planning is one of the most critical issues facing family farming today. If you haven't started working on your succession plan you may feel overwhelmed by the thought of it but the sooner you get started, the better.

This book will show you why succession planning is so important and hopefully motivate you to really look at how you are going to manage your farm operation in the future so that it is sustainable and economically viable – and that your family remains on good terms.

This is a practical guide to farm succession planning, written by farmers for farming families. By reading this book you will be able to:

- Understand the succession planning process

- Estimate how much money you need to retire comfortably

- Communicate effectively with your family to minimise conflict

- Harness a team of professionals to help you

- Deal with fairness and equity issues

- Identify the right time to transition out of the farming business

- Develop the next generation to ensure success

We were motivated to write this book because of the dire situation many of our friends were facing because they either had no succession plan at all or if they did have one, it wasn't working for them. We want to help as many farming families as possible to avoid the suffering that comes through poor succession planning.

We recommend you first read through the whole book so that you can see what's involved in the succession planning process. We have included case studies between each chapter. Many of these case studies demonstrate the dangers of not planning for succession. One of them even made us cry when we reread it but don't worry, it's not all doom and gloom - we have also included some positive ones to show you that there is light at the end of the tunnel.

We have to apologise in advance that some of the chapters are much drier than others. We have tried to make them as interesting as possible but unless you're an accountant, you're probably not going to get too excited about the topic of business structures however, it's still critical to have at least a basic understanding of this topic.

After you have read through the book, share it with other members of your family (or buy them their own copy and give it to them as a gift). Use this book to help get the dialogue started.

We will be honest, the hardest step is getting started. Talk about succession planning in your family. Then come back to the book and think about the process for your family and take action. Call a family meeting, start generating ideas and gather a team of professionals to support you. Please, do not leave it until it's too late.

We were blessed to have a transition that was relatively smooth and trouble free but that isn't the case for many families. We share Nick's personal story as a fourth generation farmer next, so you can see how it worked for us.

*Ayesha & Nick*

# Nick's Farming Story

*We want to share Nick's farming story here for you to read so that you can understand his background on the land and how succession planning worked in his family.*

I'm the third child of four children and youngest son of William and Yvonne Shady. I have an older brother Chris, an older sister Sarah and a younger sister Pru. William (or Bill as he's been known most of his life) has lived at the family property, Avenir, all his life. His father Thomas purchased the original property in 1938, some of which was owned by the family of former Liberal Premier of Victoria, Sir Henry Bolte.

My grandfather, Thomas, grew up near Coleraine, not far from Hamilton in western Victoria. He left the family farm as he was not fond of milking cows. He worked around Warracknabeal up until the great depression. He then worked with his brother near Narrandera in NSW for his keep during the depression years.

He came back to Warracknabeal and leased ground in a partnership with his former employer. After a good season, Thomas looked for some land of his own to ensure that he had somewhere that he could build an asset. He looked at a place near Waubra and then settled on the 333 acres near Skipton. After seeing the issues during dry times, Thomas wanted somewhere with a more reliable rainfall.

Thomas married Ella Barr later in life, in 1940. Bill was born in 1941 and was their only child. Bill grew up on the farm and went to school in Skipton and then spent his secondary years at boarding school in Ballarat. When he finished secondary school, Bill came home to work on the farm with his parents. Bill fell in love and married Yvonne Cutter from Ballarat in April 1964.

My childhood was quite a happy and busy one. We always helped around the farm and during school holidays we helped with shearing, harvesting or planting crops. In the '70s and early '80s chemicals were not widely used in agriculture and the paddocks were cultivated and then harrowed to get a fine seedbed and to kill the weeds. There were plenty of occasions when I sat on tractors harrowing or using offset harrows to prepare a seedbed.

The highlight was when I got to drive the Massey 65 as it had a cab and a radio with headphones. My earliest memory of driving a tractor was driving the International AW6 when Dad (Bill) would start me off with the harrows in the tractor. The only way to stop the tractor was to turn it off with the key as I was not strong enough to push the clutch in.

Helping dad was one of those things kids did after school. Chris was at boarding school at the time that I was at primary school. Chris came home on weekends and did plenty of hours on the tractor. He was at boarding school with sons of farmers from the Mallee in Victoria, so he was quickly introduced to cropping. Chris likes to grow crops; he has always been able to grow good crops and likes the challenges of farming.

Another memory of my early years was in 1979 when Chris was harvesting oats with the John Deere 55. Mum and Dad were away and an electrical fault caused a fire on the header. I can remember the fire brigade arriving to put the fire out but that was also the day that Pru got the scar over her eye!

The header was irreparable so Dad and I went on a road trip to find another header as machinery was not as abundant then as it is these days. On the way, we stayed at Dad's uncle's farm near Narrandera and I was amazed at their machinery. They always had a near-new header and the John Deere 7720 was massive (to a nine year old anyway). We ended up buying a second hand New Holland 8080 from Peel Valley machinery in Tamworth for $32,500.

This purchase seemed to increase the percentage of cropping on the farm. Chris left school in 1982 and started to grow different crops, other than oats for livestock. He grew wheat, sunflowers, rapeseed (early canola) and also linseed, which suited the late spring rains that Skipton receives. Chris purchased a new tractor in 1984, a John Deere 4040, soon after he got a 24 row International 511 seed combine. The farm purchased an old sprayer and then purchased one of the earliest Gold Acres sprayers.

Innovation was increasing in agriculture and I can remember our city cousins coming out to the farm and being amazed at the sight of Dad towing the sprayer and harrows at the same time to incorporate the Treflan, so that Chris could sow straight behind the newly sprayed paddock. Dad and Chris had a terrific linseed crop in 1985 and this was enough to get a deposit for some land.

We have been fortunate that Bill and Yvonne always trusted their children to run their farm. Chris worked hard and got the rewards he deserved. We were always involved in income decisions as well as the expenditure of the business. Chris and Bill also worked very hard and improved the genetics of the self-replacing merino flock and used the cropping for pasture improvement. At an early age, our parents were able to give some control of the business to their sons. This is a great opportunity for any child and this is when the succession plan really needs to start.

In late 1996, Chris, with the help of our parents, purchased a property just out of Lake Bolac using the money from the linseed crop for a deposit. 444 acres of land with good drainage was purchased in Chris's name. The farm was running as a sheep farm and had good improvements.

At the clearing sale on the property, Chris purchased most of the wether portion of the sheep. In 1987-88, wool prices rose quite quickly. The wool clip was about 40% higher than budgeted when the farm was purchased and it was good to be in the right place as wool was very profitable and the farm was producing many bales of quality merino wool.

The wool boom did not last; as supply increased, the prices dropped. The Australian Wool Corporation was in charge of the reserve price scheme whereby if the price was not made for the wool at auction, the wool was purchased by the AWC to put a floor in the market. The price of the scheme during the boom was at 870 cents per kg but it moved back to 700 cents in 1990. Later, it was discovered that the AWC was purchasing up to 60% of all offerings in spring 1989.

I left school in November 1988, a 17 year old who thought that he knew everything. I had no plan and didn't want to go to Agricultural College (where I had been accepted). I was always keen on finance and I was fortunate to apply for and be accepted as a batch clerk at the NAB Skipton Branch. I started the job in January 1989.

I was too young to drive at the time, so my parents would drive me the five kilometres to and from work each day. I got my motorcycle licence at seventeen and three quarters and my car licence at eighteen. I had a great time that year. I was working and earning a wage. I was learning on the job and gained more skills in that year than many trainees learnt over four years in big branches.

While I was at the bank, I saw how people looked after their finances and how important it was to be in control over your own situation. I saw what the 18% interest rate from the Hawke/Keating years did to businesses that were not well run or capitalised. One other thing I noticed was that farmers built capital from buying land and paying for that land to then build more assets.

In November, I had my holidays and I went for a drive to visit some house mates from boarding school who were working and living in Queensland. During those two weeks, I decided that I had a great opportunity to work with my family on the farm and build our futures. So I spoke to my parents and my brother about my career and we decided that it would be in everyone's best interests for me to leave the bank and work on the farm. The farm size at that time was just over 2,000 acres, running nearly 7,000 sheep.

With sheep there are always issues with lice, footrot, wet weather during lambing, wet hay, poor autumn breaks and finding labour for shearing and crutching. The biggest issue, however, was the price of wool at that time.

On the 11th of February, 1991 (about the time I finished with NAB), the Reserve Wool Price Scheme was suspended until the end of June 1991. When the wool sales resumed without the floor price, the price dropped 40% to an Eastern Market Indicator (EMI) price of 428 cents per kg.

The Reserve Price Scheme was therefore cancelled for good in June 1991, with the AWC owing $2.8 Billion and holding 4.7 million bales of wool. (This had been funded by woolgrowers and the Australian taxpayer.) The all-time low for the EMI was on the 30th of April, 1993 at 412 cents per kg. It took the AWC until the 9th of August, 2001 to sell the last bales of wool from the stockpile, most of which was sold at a loss from the levels it had been purchased at.

As you can probably tell, the early '90s were tough on the agricultural sector. Businesses that had purchased land during the wool boom found that, in some circumstances, the land prices devalued quickly. With the reduction in income, due to the lower price of the wool, some people had to sell land to reduce their debt.

At this time, we were offered and purchased (in Chris's name) a parcel of land near the other property at Lake Bolac. This property had some swamp ground that often flooded if it got wet but it also had some good banks that grew very good crops. The decision in the early '90s to do more cropping for income purposes, rather than for stockfeed and pasture improvement reasons, saw our enterprise grow quickly.

I gained my heavy combination truck licence so that we could do all our own freight and we purchased a prime mover and a couple of trailers to cart our stock and grain to markets. We were early adopters of canola in the western districts and there wasn't a great storage network for the grain so I took the canola that we grew at Lake Bolac to Millicent in South Australia. I would do one load a day but sometimes Chris and the New Holland 8080 couldn't harvest 25 tons of canola a day.

All the machinery was being purchased in the partnership at that time and there were discussions about how to protect all the partners. Avenir was owned by Mum and Dad, Chris owned the Lake Bolac properties and all the partners shared ownership of the machinery and stock. The discussion had been brought up about a plan for the future because at the time, we only had basic income protection that would cover us if one partner got sick or injured.

Also around this time, we were given the name of a business planner/succession expert in Warrnambool. We had our appointment and sat and discussed the issues together, then he also spoke to the partners separately for a short time.

He disagreed about the amount of control that Chris and I had over the business and thought that we shouldn't have any part in the partnership, "as most young blokes are likely to get girls pregnant and then cause issues with financial settlements."

This was quite a different outcome from what I had expected. Instead of setting a path towards succession and future planning, the planner was telling our parents to take back control and pay their boys wages only.

This caused some issues at home. We were all working and living together and I assumed that we were one family unit. I didn't actually really own anything at that stage and I felt that I could be at risk of being one of the family farming statistics where you work all your life for the potential of gaining an inheritance from your parents when they pass away.

We spoke about the meeting and the issues that it raised, usually at meal times. It was agreed that the next farm purchase was to be in my name, which mainly came from my determination to buy a house in Skipton so that I could start my asset building.

**We never went back to Warrnambool for a follow up meeting with the planner. It was many years later when we actually worked out a succession plan and it took many years of work and discussion to finalise the plan we have in place today.**

We invested in machinery during the '90s that suited our farming operation and practices; we purchased new harvesters, tractors, sprayers, silos and finally an airseeder. We purchased my farm in 1996; 524 acres located 25kms south east of Avenir and this is where I lived after I moved out of home.

Being educated in the bank, I had a fair knowledge of computers and I gradually started to take over the bookwork, firstly paying monthly accounts and invoicing. I had always been good with numbers, so I found it relatively easy to take on the bookwork; this was our model for efficiency as members of the family did the tasks that they specialised in.

Also in the late '90s, there was a big push by the banks into agriculture. There were now agri-business lenders that only dealt with farmers. With the increasing size of family operations, the farms needed more capital expenditure; machinery finance was once only handled by really big operators like CNH Capital. Esanda and other smaller financiers such as Corporate Finance were only used to purchase other machinery brands when those companies didn't have their own financial services providers linked to their own brand.

The banks identified the need to provide the lease/hire purchase products that modern farmers take for granted in their farming businesses. It is very hard to pay cash outright for any machinery purchase and it allows the business to pay for the machine at a set interest rate and payment amount. The ability to use these methods to increase the size of plant and machinery has seen farms getting bigger as they can operate over a larger area and therefore increase production.

Our operation purchased another 1,000 acres, 10kms south of Avenir, in 2001 in both Chris's and my name. This was purchased solely as a grain growing property. Fortunately we had sold some of our own wool stockpile to fund the deposit and the farm was purchased under a vendor term agreement. These types of deals normally work when the purchaser has 50% deposit and the vendor holds the title of the land until the whole balance is paid out. This allows the vendor to get interest on the remaining 50%, normally at better than term deposit rates, and the purchaser delays paying the stamp duty on transfer until the vendor term is paid out.

At this time, we purchased a bed-former that made two metre centred raised beds. For efficiency, we also purchased a GPS system and base station, which we still use today. The size of the operation and geographic locations of all farms (80kms) began to cause some issues and the constant travelling between farms made the timing of planting and harvesting more difficult. We tried using contractors at harvest time but with little success as the grain handling and marketing became impossible with the increased pressure. We had the right sized machinery for our operation but couldn't find the right operators that were as reliable or efficient as ourselves, the owners of the business.

Our local Ballarat based accounting firm became our sounding board for business development and succession planning. We had the correct structure in place for our farming business and we started a self-managed super fund that held non-farm investments only.

Around that time we all decided that we needed to sort out the succession plan and both of my sisters lived close enough so that we could discuss the issues. We spoke to our accountant and he said that it needed to be fair and needed to be linked with the estate plan of our parents. It has been claimed that as long as each parent has given something to each sibling in their estate, the estate should be safe from any action by a child who may think they have not been fairly treated.

As Bill had no real cash assets solely in his name, only land, the issue was how to set up a succession plan that linked in his estate plan at the same time. I suggested that the boys purchase the property from our parents which would free up cash for them but give them no link to the property that they had lived on all their lives. We didn't want Bill and Yvonne to leave the farm and their community so, with the help of our team which involved our accountant, solicitor and banker, we came up with something that would potentially work and keep everyone happy.

Bill and Yvonne would move some of the farmland into the existing farm-based super fund so that Chris and I would be the beneficiaries when that super fund is wound up. In return, that farm-based super fund would pass on cash and investments that were already in the fund into another super fund and the two girls would be the beneficiaries of that super fund when it is wound up. The control of the "daughter's super fund" was to be run by Bill and Yvonne solely, so there would be no issue when Chris or myself made decisions that affected the end value of that super fund.

This gave Chris and I certainty and motivation, knowing that the succession plan and the estate plan were linked. We also had the security of knowing that Bill and Yvonne still owned where they lived and were still the drivers of the family. At that time, Chris was living on the 1,000 acre property and had gotten married. I was single and although I was happy enough, I felt something was missing. I had a good life and travelled overseas in my early 30s, as most people do in their early 20s.

We were advised to look seriously at life insurance so we had a couple of meetings regarding what would happen if Chris or I were injured or passed away. As we only had the farm assets and some investments it would be hard to give Chris's wife security for her and her children if Chris passed away.

After a quick discussion about how much the premium for half the farm was, for each of us to insure each other, we decided to purchase another farming property near Lismore (1,100 acres) one block in my name and the other in Chris and his wife's name (Karen). The concept was that for the cost of the life insurance premiums we could partially pay for another farm and if one of us was injured or passed away, the farm could be sold to pay off debts or buy a house for the spouse with enough money left for the education of the children.

Our off-farm investments at the time were going ahead very well and we had a considerable amount invested in shares that gave us some capital gains tax headaches. Looking back at this, I regret that this money was not brought back in to pay off land and keep investing in the farm expansion.

The 2008-2009 GFC (Global Financial Crisis) really took the gloss off a very well-run business. Our shares were highly geared and therefore, without sufficient monitoring, our nest egg had really suffered. After a very tough season and harvest in 2008, we decided to stop farming together as a family at the start of 2009. At this time, I also met my future wife, Ayesha Hilton.

The most positive thing about having a succession plan in place was the idea that we could separate and keep farming on our own. Chris and I had the farmland in our own names so we did a swap of names on titles to get the farms in our own names so we could get the security we needed for the bank to split the money that we owed jointly. The plant and equipment was divided according to what I needed, what Chris needed, what belonged to Bill and Yvonne and what was to be sold.

This was a fairly difficult and time consuming job but with the help of a valuer it was made easier as Chris and I were agreeable about what everything was worth. Bill and Yvonne's farm at Avenir is still leased by Chris, as he also leases the land that is held by the super fund. As most of the cash that was put into the "daughter's super fund" came from the farming business and the farmland borrowings, there was considerable debt to be divided. Chris and I took on this debt which left Bill and Yvonne free of debt, as we were the ones that benefited from using their capital to get started.

In a perfect world we would have done things differently, especially if we knew the date we were going to discontinue farming together. The split of a working partnership this complex should be planned if possible; our split was hard work emotionally and looking back I wonder how we managed to get that year's crop in the ground. I think a three to five year plan would be the optimum time to plan this, so you can work out the time, how to split machinery, land and debts and so that everyone is in a position to continue farming with little disruption.

I am glad that my parents trusted their sons to run the business and look after their interests. At a young age we were given the reins and also the financial responsibility and we were fortunate to be in the right place at the right time. People say that the harder you work, the luckier you are! By gaining control of the business at that time we were able to expand the size of the enterprise and therefore invest in the capital to improve efficiencies which were needed to upscale the business, as fixed costs continue to rise.

Family farming always has issues regarding who gets what, whether it is how the income is distributed for families that work on the farm or own the farm or in some circumstances, don't farm. Financial independence in farming is rare at an early age and the longer you work together the harder it is to become independent. I find that financial independence really only occurs when you run your own business.

I no longer live full time on the farming property as I do not enjoy the stress of living where I work. I find it hard to cope when the crops are being flooded or conversely when it doesn't rain. Mental health is a huge issue on the land and with huge investments in growing crops, the risks add up.

In 2010, I had the worst year since I have been farming; not a drought but constant rain and cold weather. The crops that grew were flooded just before my wedding to my wife Ayesha in August. I replanted up until November with late crops such as barley. This, in turn with a very wet harvest, made the income look very poor and I had to borrow more money to cover the payments for my machinery which I had purchased the year before.

Ayesha and I lived in Ballarat with her daughter Grace and Ayesha's father, Shaun, when we got married. We moved into our dream house in Ballarat in 2011 when we found out that we were having our much anticipated baby.

Spencer William Hilton Shady was born at home on the 27th of December, 2011. I drive out to the farm when I need to, as I have the freedom of not owning any livestock to manage, and I stay at the farmhouse when I am working late or need to get jobs done such as planting, spraying or harvesting.

I managed to use my 20+ years of business experience to gain an MBA from Federation University (formally Ballarat University). Since gaining this important educational experience, I look at the way people do business differently than before. I realise that before the MBA, I didn't identify such things as Sustained Competitive Advantage. I realise now that our business was built on the advantage of being a close family unit, which worked and communicated very well together.

I am currently cropping 1,550 acres of my own property and nearly 600 acres of share farming. I have been working on a low input cost system for my cropping operation and I am using liquid fertilizer at planting time and using a companion crop (peas) in my canola rotation. I use wheat that is acid soil tolerant and I have gone back to some linseed to get a good weed kill or when the canola gets washed out (which happened on 200 acres this season).

I need to be able to use all my skills to sell my produce at the right time and to get the best price I can. I use wheat swaps as a forward marketing tool and for some deferred cash flow, I store some on farm. I have very good relationships with grain buyers, some of whom I have dealt with for over 20 years.

I am very lucky to be in the situation where I am financially independent but due to the GFC and other decisions, I have a heavy debt load and I am very dependent on my bank. Family farming is about creating an environment where we are proud of what we produce, proud of our land, our community and most of all our families. Without farming families, Australia would lose its rural identity.

With the changing climate of farming, I hope my story and this book will inspire others to look forward to their own future. Looking at what they would like their family, farming or not, to look like in the next ten years. Maybe it is time to look at what you want to leave behind, the many years of hard work and the legacy of your existence.

*Nick Shady*

June 2015

# What is Succession Planning & Why is it Important?

# Chapter 1:

# What is Succession Planning & Why is it Important?

*" Poor succession planning is one of the biggest challenges facing farmers across the world and it can destroy businesses and families if it's not done right. "*

### Nick Shady

What a scary topic for most families in farming – succession planning – the transitioning of control of assets and management and all the potential conflict that might come with it. Yet, in other industries, succession planning is simply a part of normal business management and that's how it needs to be in family farming.

So what exactly is succession planning?

*Succession planning is a process that occurs over time where the* **knowledge, skills, labour, management, control and ownership of the farm business occurs between stakeholders** *(usually the retiring generation and the successor generation).*

It involves the growth and preservation of the business and ultimately the transfer of assets and control to the next generation.

Each family farming business is unique in terms of how they run their farming operation, the family structure, the relationship dynamics and each family member's dreams and expectations.

While succession planning may seem fraught with danger, it is far more hazardous in the long run to do nothing at all. You probably worked out long ago, if you're still farming, that sticking your head in the sand doesn't solve anything.

If you're like many farming families, the thought of starting the succession planning process is challenging due to the risk of conflict or disagreement but the sooner you start planning, the better it will be for everyone involved.

With a comprehensive succession plan in place, you and your family will know what to expect when circumstances change. And things do change. We get married, we have children, we experience loss and injury and the business cycles through good years and bad years, great markets and poor markets.

There are so many variables in farming – you almost have to be a bit of a gambler to handle the stress! However, you can be prepared for many of the possibilities with a sound succession plan.

## THE REASONS WHY FARMING FAMILIES AVOID SUCCESSION PLANNING

*" If succession planning issues were well understood by farmers, there would be more plans in place... "* [1]

Succession planning is an almost taboo subject for many farming families; it brings up a lot of fear and angst and often bitter resentment. It's understandable why only about 50% of farming businesses have a succession plan in place.

If you've been avoiding succession planning, no doubt the following will sound familiar to you.

Here are the top five reasons farmers avoid succession planning:

### 1. Fear of Conflict

Fear of conflict and arguments is probably the biggest reason why people avoid succession planning. Farming is a unique type of business in that you are working with your family members, so avoiding conflict with the people you live and work with is important. There are ways of navigating the succession planning process to minimise conflict and increase family harmony.

---

1    Betker, T. (2014). *Farm Succession Planning: A Workback Approach.*

## 2. Too Hard

Many families feel that the whole thing is just too hard. Succession planning is a big process. It takes a lot of effort and resources and there's no quick fix. You have to develop your plan, implement it and then review and modify it as needed. You will see later in the book that there is a lot of work involved in succession planning but all the elements of the plan help you build a stronger business while looking after the needs and aspirations of family members.

## 3. Don't Know How

Governments around the western world have put a lot of money into programs to help farmers develop and implement succession plans. But for all this effort, the number of farmers with succession plans has not shown much of an increase. Yes, succession planning can be complex but there are plenty of resources available to you.

## 4. Bad Past Experiences

If the head of the family farm has had a bad experience with succession planning with their own parents or family, it has probably left a bitter taste in their mouth and given them a bloody good reason to stay clear of succession planning. If managed well, a succession plan can avoid this type of bitterness.

## 5. Not Their Job

Who has responsibility for the succession plan? That's a good question. Some may say it's the job of the head of the farm. But what if they are unwilling to bring it up, then what? A succession plan is the responsibility of all members of the farming family. It might take one person in the family to have the courage to say, "Hey, we really need a succession plan." Someone has to say it, why not you?

As you can see, all these reasons have truth to them but they shouldn't put you off succession planning. As you will see below, succession planning is now more important than ever.

# WHY SUCCESSION PLANNING IS MORE IMPORTANT THAN EVER

*"One of the most pressing issues is the ageing population of farmers. In 2011, the median age of farmers was 53 years, compared with 40 years for people in other occupations."* [2]

Family farming has changed much over the last hundred years. Today, succession planning is more important than ever for a number of reasons.

Here are the top five reasons why succession is so important for today's farming families:

## 1. Living & Working Longer

Farmers are now farming longer than ever as many are healthier and living longer. This means that the next generation are having to wait longer to take over the day to day management and running of the farm. On average, women live longer than men and this means that often, the mother will outlive the father and then either she controls the farming assets or the children have to provide for her security.

## 2. Farm Income Can't Support Multiple Families

Many farming parents have more than one child working and living on the farm, yet many farms do not make enough income to support multiple families. Without capital expansion, and probably taking on more debt, there is simply not enough to go around for the next generation.

## 3. Carving-Up the Farm Reduces Economic Viability

Dividing up a farm into equal portions for the next generation may seem fair but it also reduces the on-going economic viability of the farming enterprise. Everyone may get their fair share of acres but then no one has enough to make a living. Also, the economy of scale required to generate enough income from farming, with tighter margins and higher land values, makes buying out siblings very difficult.

---

2    Farming Ahead (2013). *Research Report: Food Security – Safe is better than sorry.*

## 4. Changes in Expectations of Off-Farm Siblings

In the past, the oldest farming son was the natural beneficiary but now other non-farming children are seeking equality with their farming siblings. The next generation does not agree with the oldest child automatically getting the farm and the others siblings missing out and they are often not afraid to stake their claim.

## 5. Generational Differences

There is now a greater difference in attitude between the older farming generation and the next generations. The older farmers have a history of working longer and harder. The new generation of farmers look to technology to work smarter. They want to use technology to increase productivity and income. They also have a difference in values, they want to spend more time with their families and work less. They value freedom, independence and financial security.

# THE 9 KEY BENEFITS OF SUCCESSION PLANNING

*" The most difficult thing is the decision to act.*
*The rest is tenacity. "*

### Amelia Earhart

While you may be fearful of starting the succession planning process, there are so many benefits for you and your family in developing a fair succession plan for all those involved.

Let's have a look at the nine key benefits of a sound succession plan:

## 1. Open Discussion & Communication

Succession planning provides the opportunity to discuss key areas of concern and future aspirations in advance. This can help reduce the risk of future disagreements and tension in the family.

## 2. Risk Management & Prevention

By understanding what strategies you need to have in place now, before things get bad, you can prevent a lot of issues from ever arising. As a family you can discuss and analyse potential and future risks and implement strategies to mitigate these risks. Importantly, you can create a business structure that is responsive to the needs and desires of each family member.

## 3. Family Harmony

The family can move beyond thinly veiled resentment, jealousy, anger, sadness or other emotions that are alive in the family dynamic. It also takes the pressure off parents to "sort it all out" as it is a shared process.

## 4. Framework for Working with Your Family

Working with family can be tough. By having a succession plan, you effectively have a framework and plan for managing the complexities of working with your own family. This can reduce the misunderstandings and resentment that can build over time.

## 5. Direction & Clarity

Through open dialogue, each family member can get clarity and direction about their future. This is very empowering! It also determines the future direction of the farming enterprise because everyone knows what each of the other family members wants and decisions can be made based on this direction.

## 6. More Security for Family Members

Succession planning can help each family member feel secure in their future as they know their needs and desires have been considered. Lack of security is one of those things that most stresses people out. So this is critical to your wellbeing and that of your family.

## 7. Less Stress & Anxiety

Feeling more secure in your future and in your finances, as well as your continued role in the family farm, has such a huge impact on stress and anxiety levels. One of the biggest problems in rural areas is suicide. While there are many reasons for suicide, it is not hard to imagine the despair that many feel in the face of an uncertain future.

## 8. Increased Motivation & Enthusiasm

When everyone feels that they have been listened to and their needs are being met, they feel more excited about the farming business. Knowing their stake in the future provides strong motivation for the younger generation to contribute to the farm.

## 9. Greater Profitability & Providing for Retirement

Having a good strategic succession plan in place will build greater wealth for you and your family. It will also save you lots of heartache and wasted money in the long run. If done early enough, succession planning will allow you to generate income for the retirement of those leaving the farm, as well as develop income to support the incoming generation. This will ensure the viability of the farming business.

# BUT WHAT IF YOU HAVE A VERBAL SUCCESSION PLAN?

Many families have a verbal agreement about succession plans. Verbal succession plans happen in family farming because the people involved share a relationship of trust.

On the one hand, it seems quite reasonable to operate on a verbal agreement in an extended family; however, the problem with verbal agreements is that circumstances can change.

People's recollections become distorted over time and this can often result in misunderstandings that cause relationships to break down and possibly the breakdown of the farming operation as well.

Given the complex nature of family farming today, it is necessary to have a documented plan along with the appropriate legal documents to support the plan.

*You might trust your family but it's still better to have everything written down so that everyone is protected.*

## PRIORITISING SUCCESSION PLANNING

As you can see, a lot of misery, uncertainty and conflict can occur if you don't have a succession plan. Having a sound succession plan in place, that is reviewed regularly, will enable your family farming business to be more sustainable in the long term, with family members happier, more secure and more motivated. This means your family can be happier and hopefully more profitable.

One of the most common issues with succession planning is the time it takes to get the plan completed. It is important to realise early on, that succession planning is a process that requires a significant amount of time to work through.

We have seen many families start the succession planning process and then without any accountability or deadlines in place, the whole thing falls in a heap. It's easy to lose focus as seemingly more important or urgent farm management issues arise and take precedence over succession planning.

In the book, Seven Habits of Highly Successful People by Stephen R Covey[3], he has four quadrants for time management for organising your priorities. It differentiates between activities that are important and those that are urgent.

Important activities are integral to achieving your goals. Urgent activities demand your immediate attention but are often associated with achieving someone else's goals.

The normal tendency is to focus on urgent things, and these are often important as well, but there needs to be time set aside to focus on important things *before* they become urgent.

Generally, succession planning will probably fit into the important but not urgent category – that is, until it becomes urgent! It's best to deal with your succession plan before it becomes urgent.

The earlier you start your succession planning process, the better. There will always be urgent and important things you have to do on your farm but you still need to put aside time for important but not urgent things, such as succession planning.

---

3    Covey, S. (1999). *Living the 7 Habits.*

# Case Study 1:

# Husband Goes into Nursing Home

*" Greg and I had retired to the local town, leaving our son to run the family farm. We still owned some farm assets but they weren't bringing in much money. When Greg got too sick to stay at home, I had to find the money to pay for the nursing home. We didn't get funding for his place in the home because of our assets and I had to come up with the money to pay for Greg's care. "*

With an aging population, more and more farming families will face the challenge of caring for the older generation. Farming families are often asset rich and cash flow poor. These assets can mean that families don't get the government support that other families with the same income would get. Often farm assets need to be sold off to fund the care of the parents.

## Janet's Story

Greg and I lived and worked on our farm for more than 40 years. We farmed with our son Graham for 15 years. When Graham got married, we decided to retire to the local town. We gave Graham the house block on the farm that we had lived on so that he and his wife could raise their family there.

We were still in a farming partnership with Graham and we had a small residual income coming in through this partnership. Greg would still help Graham at the farm as it was his passion and he couldn't stay away from the farm.

A few years after we moved to town, Greg became increasingly unwell. It was hard to see this vibrant and hardworking man become so incapacitated. There came a point where I could no longer take care of him by myself at home.

We made the difficult decision to move Greg to a nursing home. I hadn't realised how hard it would be to pay for Greg's care. Of course, I wanted him to be well taken care of and I would do whatever it took to make sure that was the case.

The cost of the nursing home was very high for us because we had the farm assets. Even though we had little cash flow, this didn't make any difference to the cost. It was so stressful trying to come up with the money to pay for Greg's care. In the end, I had to sell the farm land to pay for Greg's care. Thankfully, Graham was able to purchase the land so that it stayed in the family.

I'm in good health and I could easily live for another 15 to 20 years. I am not sure I have the money to live that long because I've used up all our savings to pay for Greg's care.

## LESSONS LEARNED

- You need to be realistic about the future needs of aging family members
- You need to understand how your assets will impact the cost of nursing home care
- You either need to reduce your assets before care is required or to have the money available to fund nursing home care if it is required

# The Dangers of NOT Undertaking Succession Planning

# Chapter 2:

# The Dangers of NOT Undertaking Succession Planning

*" It is really difficult to measure the cost of deferring planning for succession. But, for most farms, there very likely will be a cost at some point in time. The ultimate cost can be a farm that cannot be transitioned to the next generation."* [4]

There are numerous dangers in avoiding the succession planning process. If you've been around farming long enough, you will have noticed what happens when there is no clear succession plan. You may have seen this with friends, relatives, or other people in your farming community. And you'll want to avoid these dangers yourself!

The top three dangers of NOT undertaking succession planning are:

## 1.  Family Discord

When there is no open discussion and formal plan in place, it can give rise to family discord and a serious breakdown in relationships. Everyday exchanges between family members can be tense. There can be a lot of bitching behind closed doors, followed by a polite but tense veneer in everyday conversations. This is a stressful and unpleasant way to live.

## 2.  Lack of Opportunities

Without a plan, the next generation working on the farm may not have opportunities for growing their asset base, having a good income for their own families (and often their wife having to work off farm to supplement farm income), and for implementing new management strategies.

---

4    Betker, T. (2014). *Farm Succession Planning: A Workback Approach.*

### 3. Squandering of Assets

Many farms have been in the same family for generations, growing as they expand and buying more land over time. These assets can be easily jeopardised if there is no succession plan in place. This means that you could work on your family farm for most of your adult life and not have a good inheritance after all your hard work.

*Don't stick your head in the sand!*
*The problems only get worse if you ignore them.*

*"To me, farm succession is a dirty word. Farm succession is something that makes me quiver when I think of it. To me, all it means is arguments, squabbles, bitterness resentment. Every time it comes up in conversation there's always so much negativity about it. I don't think my in-laws even know that there is such a thing as succession planning. I just can't fight anymore, I've just run out of the energy and caring to fight anymore."*

Anonymous Woman from ABC Rural interview [5]

## THE 5DS THAT COULD SPELL DISASTER FOR YOUR FARM

You know that disaster can strike at any time if you're a farmer. And in family farming life, there are five major events that can totally rock your world and potentially destroy your business. The potential of these disasters alone should motivate you to work on your succession plan.

Here are the 5Ds that could impact your farming business: [6]

### 1. Death

A farm would continue to operate if a spouse dies who does not work on the farm. But what happens if the person who manages the farm and does much of the labour dies? This would totally change the way the farm is managed

---

5   ABC Rural, (2014). *Succession planning: the good, the bad and the ugly.*

6   University of Wisconsin - Center for Dairy Profitability, (2014). *5Ds.*

and operated. Life insurance can provide protection for families and the business in the event of death and is worth looking at for your family.

## 2. Disability

Farming is by nature a risky business and accidents can easily happen on farms. According to ABS statistics, farming is one of the most dangerous jobs in the country. You probably know someone who has been seriously injured on their farm. Sometimes these injuries are short-term and the person can recover enough to continue working on the farm.

Other times, these injuries create permanent disabilities that mean the person can't work on the farm like they used to. Whatever the case, you still need to have a plan in place to deal with the potential of disability. You may want to look at getting disability or income protection insurance for the key family members. Of course, prevention is critical, so having good practices in place to minimise the risk of injury and accidents is very important.

## 3. Disaster

Natural disasters happen all the time. In Australia, we are plagued with droughts, floods and fires. Mother nature can throw anything at us at any time. There are also other manmade disasters and so called acts of God that can spell disaster for your family, whether it be contaminated feed, an outbreak of disease or a plague of locusts. You need to be ready with an action plan to deal with disaster before it strikes.

## 4. Divorce

Death and taxes are inevitable, we know it. But divorce is a dirty word that we farmers would rather not talk about or plan for. As you know, as many as 50% of marriages end in divorce. According to the ABS, farming families actually have a lower rate of divorce than the national average but that doesn't mean divorce can't happen. Divorce can create a lot of problems for the farming business as you've probably seen in your own community. You can have a pre or post nuptial agreement that stipulates where assets will be distributed upon divorce which can protect the farming business in that event.

## 5. Disagreements

Farming is stressful and disagreements can really destroy a farming business. There are lots of reasons why disagreements occur. Generations might disagree on how things should be run. With multiple families involved in running the business, there will be different expectations. Circumstances change and children get married and have their own children. We work long hours in farming and this can really eat into the time we have to spend with our families and can easily cause friction between a husband and wife. The level of debt the farm is carrying will also have an impact on the stress levels in the family.

Disagreements are almost a certainty if you farm long enough but they don't need to spell disaster for your farm. Acknowledging that disagreements can happen and having strategies in place to deal with them if they arise can help.

These 5Ds pose potential risks for you and your business and should motivate you to get started on your succession plan. You need to have a written contingency plan in place to deal with these dangerous Ds if they should eventuate as they will have a big impact on your succession plan and how you transfer assets and management.

*Next we will share a case study with you that brings home just how important it is to have a plan in place in case tragedy strikes. You might need some tissues (we did when we reread it). After the case study, we will share some guiding principles to keep in mind throughout the succession planning process.*

# Case Study 2:

# Husband Dies in Farm Accident

*" It was an ordinary morning, just like any other day. Little did I know how much our lives would change in an instant. I lost my husband, our livelihood and our home because we weren't prepared. "*

If you were to die tomorrow, would your family have enough cash flow to survive until they sorted out your assets? You need to think about the potential of death and injury so that you can be prepared and your family can be taken care of.

## Kaitlin's Story

Cory and I married young and got our first farm together when we were in our early 20s. Cory grew up on a farm but didn't get along with his father, so we decided to farm on our own. We ran a 3,000 acre cropping farm with a few sheep to keep the grass down around the house.

We were carrying a lot of debt for land and machinery. Some years, when the harvest was poor, we could barely make the repayments and had to live on our overdraft. We had only a small disposable income because we wanted to pay down as much debt as possible. I was pretty good at making ends meet but it wasn't easy.

One day, while I was in town doing the grocery shopping, I got a call on my mobile from our neighbour, Les. There'd been an accident and Cory was trapped under the four wheeler motorbike. I dropped my shopping and ran to the car. I drove the 70kms back to the farm as fast as I could.

When I arrived, the police and paramedics where there and Cory was conscious but obviously in a lot of pain. The emergency services people were organising for the four wheeler to be lifted off Cory. It was agonising to watch. Cory's condition was getting worse and he was drifting in and out of consciousness. Thankfully, I was able to talk with him and reassure him for a little while.

I told him how much I loved him and that he needed to hang in there for me and the kids. He told me how much he loved me and that he was sorry, then he closed his eyes for the last time. I could tell he was gone but I couldn't believe it.

That morning, I hadn't kissed him goodbye as he left for work. I was cross with him because he'd left a mess all over the kitchen the night before and there were ants all over the benches. It's such a trivial thing to be cross about, all things considered.

When the kids got off the bus that afternoon, I had to tell them their father was dead. It was the hardest thing I ever had to do; looking into their sweet, innocent eyes and seeing the shock and confusion.

I didn't realise it at the time but not only had we lost Cory, we would also lose our home. After we buried Cory, I tried to run the farm myself. I couldn't do it all alone; I didn't know how to drive a header, a truck or even the tractor. I couldn't sow the crops. I couldn't spray them and I couldn't harvest them. I tried to get contractors in but I didn't have enough money to pay them.

I realised that I needed to sell the farm as I had no income and no way of sowing and harvesting the crops. I was stuffed. I thought it would be easy to sell the machinery and the farm but I was wrong. It took more than 12 months to get everything sold. Meanwhile, I had to go on government benefits just so that the kids and I could eat.

Until Cory died, I didn't realise that we were in such a precarious situation. We didn't have any life insurance for either of us but if we had, it would have made such a big difference.

I would have loved to have stayed on the farm but I had no money coming in. It was the hardest year of my life. I missed Cory dreadfully. He had the cheekiest grin and was always making me laugh. There hasn't been much laughter in our lives since he died.

We now live in town and I've got a job at the local supermarket. I had enough money from selling the farm to put a large deposit on a house. The kids are adjusting to their new life but they miss their dad and the farm.

## THE LESSONS

- You need to have a contingency plan in place for death and disability

- You never know when something bad will happen

- If your spouse is left to manage the farm when you die, how will they fund the extra help they need to keep the farm running or pay the debts until they can sell the farm and machinery?

- You really need disability and life insurance to ensure your family are taken care of if you die or are injured and can no longer work

# What are the Guiding Principles for Succession Planning?

# Chapter 3:

# What are the Guiding Principles for Succession Planning?

*" The law of harvest is to reap more than you sow. Sow an act, and you reap a habit. Sow a habit and you reap a character. Sow a character and you reap a destiny. "*

### James Allen

A detailed process, that aligns timelines and expectations and outlines what needs to be done and in what specific order, will help you manoeuvre through the minefield of succession planning. There are a number of guiding principles to keep in mind when you embark upon the succession planning journey, including:

- **Be Proactive**

    Take initiative, your decisions and actions are the primary determining factors for the effectiveness in your life. Take responsibility for your choices and the consequences that follow.

- **Begin with the End in Mind**

    Clarify what you want and have a clear vision of what you want for your family and your life.

- **Think Win-Win**

    Aim for a win-win outcome where the succession plan is as mutually beneficial for each family group as possible. Value and respect people by understanding a "win" for all is ultimately a better long-term resolution than if only one person in the situation had gotten his or her way.

- **Seek First to Understand, Then to be Understood**

  Genuinely listen to other family members so you can understand their needs. This can create an atmosphere of caring and positive problem solving as well as encouraging others to really listen to your needs too.

- **Understand that Fair is not always Equal**

  Fair and equal are not the same thing. There needs to be an understanding that fairness is more important than equality.

  *See Chapter 11: How Do You Deal with Fairness & Equity Issues?*

- **Create a Professional Support Team**

  You need the help of a professional support team to create your succession plan including accountant, lawyer, facilitator or succession planning consultant, your lender/bank, etc.

- **Don't Listen to Everyone**

  Only take advice from people who are qualified to give you advice. These are the people who have your best interests at heart and have the knowledge and expertise in the area you're talking about.

- **Be the Victor not the Victim**

  Be the Victor by taking ownership, accountability and responsibility for your actions, thoughts and emotions. Do not be a victim where you blame others, make excuses or live in denial.

## THE DO'S & DON'TS

There are a lot of things to consider when starting the succession planning process. Before you start, here is a high level reminder of the things you should do and the things you should avoid with succession planning.[7]

---

7   Rural Law Online, (2014). *Farm Succession Planning: Forum Report.*

## The Do's

We highly recommend you do the following:

- Think of succession planning as a **process** rather than an event - it takes time and effort.

- **Start planning now** – the earlier planning begins, the greater the number of options.

- **Keep the bigger picture in mind** – the long-term future of the farm.

- Maintain a **positive attitude** – it can make a huge difference as attitudes are contagious.

- Complete a **financial analysis** of the past and present farm business along with some financial projections. If your farm is not making money now, what can be done to make it profitable? Is the farm business actually viable in the long run?

- Become **educated about succession planning** — take workshops and seminars, read articles and complete self-assessment questionnaires related to succession so that you are an active participant in the planning process. (And read the rest of this book!)

- Use a **family business meeting** to open the lines of communication among family members. An objective, third-party facilitator can help ensure that the initial meetings run smoothly and everyone has an opportunity to voice their interests and concerns.

- Determine **the most important things** (values and their priorities) to each individual family member as a starting point. The business meeting mentioned above can be helpful with this.

- Figure out **each individual's personal, family and business goals**, which should be based upon their values and priorities.

- Ensure **good communication** among family members about plans, strategies and issues.

- Address the tricky issue of **fair (equitable) vs. equal division** of the farm early in the process — especially if there are off-farm family members involved.

- Prepare a **legal will** early. A will can provide guidance on how the estate should be settled.

- Generate and discuss **various options**. You can narrow these down over time but in the beginning have a big brainstorming session about possible options.

- Assemble your **team of professional advisors** (e.g. lawyer, accountant, financial planner, banker, etc.) and work with them on your succession plan.

- **Take responsibility** for development and implementation of the plan with help from your team of advisors. This is your family's plan, not the advisors. Family members have to buy into the plan for it to be successful.

- Consider the **tax implications** but don't focus solely on them as the most important thing. For example, rather than saying, "We don't want to pay any taxes," make your goal, "Transfer the farm business efficiently and effectively while considering the tax consequences and preserving as much family capital as possible."

- **Document your plan**. By writing it down, all family members see exactly what's in the plan and how it is going to be rolled out.

## The Don'ts

Do the Do's above and please try and follow the advice below:

- Don't **procrastinate** - start the process now.

- Don't **be afraid to ask questions** and listen to the answer, no matter how uncomfortable some of the answers might be.

- Don't **assume** you know what others are thinking or how they feel about the process or what they want to achieve from the succession plan. If you don't understand, clarify with questions and listen carefully.

- Don't **be afraid to share responsibilities**. Both generations need to work together to develop the best succession plan. Use a professional succession planner or facilitator if you need to.

- Don't **define life as the business**. There is more to life than work — family, friends, leisure enjoyment, sports, hobbies, etc.

- Don't **put all your eggs in one basket**. Plan ahead, think early about retirement, save and invest off-farm so that you will have some options in the future.

- Don't **rely on just one professional advisor**. Use a team of people with different skills and expertise.

By developing a comprehensive succession plan, you will help build something that will serve your family for generations to come.

*Next we will share a case study about the impact that divorce can have on a farming business and the family as a whole. After the case study, we will look at planning for your retirement (no matter what your age right now).*

# Case Study 3:

# Son Gets Divorced

*" I never expected to get divorced. I didn't realise how unhappy my wife was. When she told me she was leaving and wanted a divorce, I was shocked. I didn't realise how it would destroy the relationships with the rest of my family."*

While the farming community has a lower divorce rate than other groups in society, there are a lot of pressures on farming families that can lead to divorce. When a son divorces and he owns part of the farm, this can create real problems if he has to buy his former wife out of the business.

### Jeremy's Story

The Browns have been farming together for 15 years. There are two generations working together and they all own a share of the farming business. There's my dad Dave, who's nearly 73, my mum Mavis, who's also in her early 70s, my brother Graham and his wife April, along with me and my wife, Janine.

Janine had been unhappy living on the farm for a while. We'd been fighting all the time, mostly about money and the children's education. Janine didn't want our kids to go to boarding school, she wanted them to live at home and for us to be together as a family. I went to boarding school and it didn't do me any harm, the kids just need to toughen up, I'd tell Janine. I thought she was way too soft on them.

One day, I came home from work and I was surprised when Janine told me she was moving out and she wanted a divorce. She had her car packed and was taking the kids to her mum's house about two hours drive away. She was hurt and angry and said she couldn't take it anymore. I was stunned. I couldn't believe what was happening.

Janine wanted to make a new life for herself in town with the kids. This meant she needed money to buy a house and to support her and the children. She enrolled in a childcare course and wants to get a job when she graduates. In the meantime, she needs maintenance from me and wants her share of our assets.

I have to pay Janine for her share of the farm. Somehow, I have to come up with a shit load of money that I just don't have. The payload in farming is all in the assets, not in the cashflow.

Unfortunately, this situation has created enormous conflict between me and the rest of my family. They are resentful that they have been put in this situation and that their livelihood and financial security are at stake.

## THE LESSONS

- Any marriage, no matter how seemingly stable and loving, has the potential to end in divorce
- Divorce opens up a whole lot of problems for farming families
- Divorce and the subsequent break up of assets can mean that the farm is no longer viable
- If you don't have the cash flow to buy out the other party, you might be forced to sell your farm
- If possible, get a pre or post nuptial agreement in place to protect the farm assets from being broken up
- Family resentment and disharmony are common in this situation
- Look at off farm assets, such as those in a regional city
- Divorce causes stress as money has to be borrowed by family members to buy out the leaving party

# What's your Game Plan & Retirement Strategy?

Chapter 4:

# What's your Game Plan & Retirement Strategy?

*"Successful farm succession planning requires balancing retirement needs against inheritance."*

### Nick Shady

Life is a precious gift. It can be taken away from us at any moment and in farming, we are more aware of the balance of life and death than most other people.

Given this awareness of the fragile nature of life, what is it that you most what to achieve during your lifetime?

If you were to imagine your perfect life:

- What would it look like?
- Who would you be with?
- Where would you be?
- How would you be feeling?
- What would you be doing?

These can be hard questions to answer if you've always just plodded along in your farming career and done what is expected of you but given the precious nature of life, what is it that would give you the most contentment and sense of accomplishment?

Knowing and acknowledging your needs and desires will help you develop a game plan for your life so that you can go into the succession planning process with clarity and purpose. Everyone in the family needs their own game plan; they need to know what they want for their life.

## KEY QUESTIONS TO ASK YOURSELF

Here are some key questions you can ask yourself to get clarity about what is most important to you and your family so that you can develop a game plan and retirement strategy.

### Your Preferences

- What do you want to leave as your **legacy**?

- How do you want to **be remembered** by your family and friends when you're gone?

- Is farming what you really **want** to do?

- What do you most **enjoy** doing on the farm?

- What are you **good at but you don't enjoy**?

- What would you like to **learn** that would be useful to the business?

- How much **income** do you want to get from the business?

- Are you happy working with **siblings**?

- Have you been appropriately **remunerated** for the work you have done on the farm?

- Can the farm cater for **expected expenses** such as school fees and holidays?

### Family & Lifestyle

- What sort of **lifestyle** do you want to have?

- Where will you **educate** your children?

- Does your **partner** want to work on the farm or do something different?

- How much do you want to **work**?

- How much **holiday** time do you want to have?

## Retirement & Harvest Strategy

- When do you want to **hand over management** of the farm?
- When do you want to **hand over ownership** of the farm?
- How do you wish to **retire**?
- Where do you want to **live** after you retire?
- How will you be **supported** financially?
- What **will you do** when retired?
    - Will you travel to the farm to help? If so, how often?
    - Will you travel Australia/overseas? If so, how often?
- How can you **treat your children fairly** but **not risk the viability** of the business you have created?
- Who will have the responsibility of **paying out siblings** or children?
- Will **off farm family** members have ownership of the business and how will they be rewarded or paid out?
- Do you want any **debt** in retirement?

## Farm Management

- What would be the **ideal outcome** for the business as a result of the succession plan?
- What are the **key issues** which need to be resolved to reach an outcome that would satisfy everyone?
- What are/or will be the **terms and conditions** for family members working in the business?
- How will the **business be structured** when family members enter?
- How will **communication** flow to family members both inside and outside the business?
- How will family members inside the business be educated and given **professional development**?
- What is the process for **decision making**?
- What happens in the event of **illness, disability or death**?

- How and when will **responsibility for management** of the business be passed on?

## And if you take no action?

- What are the **consequences** of not formulating a succession plan for the business and your family?

Answering these questions will give you greater clarity about what you want to get out of your succession plan.

*"For many current owners, the idea of continuing the legacy is part of their dream but they want a graceful exit and need to establish a sound retirement, or semi-retirement, income."[8]*

## HARVEST STRATEGY: PLANNING FOR YOUR RETIREMENT

*" Due to a lack of succession planning, many people find themselves in their fifties still working for their parents with little farm management input and no financial autonomy. Living on a basic wage with no freedom. "*

Nick Shady

For many farmers, retirement often commences (or is thrust upon a parent by a frustrated farming child) with little or no cash in reserve, nowhere else to live but on the farm and no regular income sources. You want to avoid this situation. To do this, you need to plan now for retirement, not wait until the 11th hour.

A harvest strategy is similar to what you currently do – you plant the crops to reap the rewards. So looking towards your retirement as the "harvest," ask yourself what you want for that phase of your life and how are you going to get it.

There are a number of things you need to do to cultivate your harvest for your retirement. First, you need to work out how much money you need to fund your

---

8    Betker, T. (2014). Farm Succession Planning: A Workback Approach

retirement and then put strategies in place to generate the funds you need to retire, when and how you want.[9]

Some of the strategies farmers can put in place to create financial security for their retirement include:

- Maintain an **income only interest** in the farming business

- Build up **off-farm assets** such as shares and investments

- Create a **self-managed super fund**

- **Reduce debt** in good years

- Increase **land holdings** to grow asset and income base

Many older farmers will need to rely on government pensions and related benefits for their retirement. However, these are not guaranteed for future generations and they do not provide enough money to have a decent standard of living.

Even if you're nowhere near retiring, it's never too soon to put strategies in place to ensure you have the money to fund your retirement.

## Estimate how much money you will need to fund your retirement

Let's assume you want to retire at 65 and you want to have an income to age 100, assuming a rate of return of 5.0% (net of all fees) and no aged pension, you would need the following capital sums:

| Income Per Annum | Capital Required |
|---|---|
| $25,000 | $500,000 |
| $50,000 | $1,000,000 |
| $75,000 | $1,500,000 |
| $100,000 | $2,000,000 |

---

9    Disclaimer: Please speak to a qualified financial planner or other relevant professional when making financial decisions.

As you can see, you would need quite a lot of capital to fund a very modest retirement. This is without reinvesting in the capital growth of your investment, so your capital can be eroded if invested in shares and the market goes down.

## Maintain an income only interest in the farm

In your succession plan, you may choose to retain an income only interest in the farm when you retire. This can be achieved through beneficial interest in a trust or through a non-management interest in a partnership. However, the danger with this approach is that it may erode the capital available for the operation of the farm.

Also, as the financial needs of the younger generation grow, either the income from the farm must grow to match changing needs or other sources of income must be found.[10]

## Build up your off-farm assets

Asset building, whether off-farm or on-farm, is important in planning for your financial future. The advantage of buying off-farm assets in your own name is that they are separate from the farm assets, which gives you the flexibility to retire, move away or sell the assets when you want.

The most common types of off-farm assets include a house in a regional city, a beach house, investment properties, as well as share portfolios and cash term deposits. Speak with your financial advisor about the best strategy for you.

## Fund your own pension through superannuation

You can fund your own superannuation pension through contributions to a super fund. Superannuation fund contributions are tax deductible and you get to keep more of your income to assist with growing your assets.

If you want more control over your superannuation planning and assets, you may want to look at setting up a self-managed super fund (SMSF). These are quite expensive to set up and run and require a high level of investment and

---

10 Fleming Muntz Solicitors (2008). *Succession and Estate Planning for Country Clients.*

expertise. However, you would have greater control against your investments and you may be able to borrow against it for asset building.

Where there are no farming successors, you could lease out your farmland on retirement to generate regular income. If you do this, consider using a SMSF to hold land as it offers enormous income tax advantages because of the low tax rate and the fact that once pensions are commenced upon the member's retirement, the superannuation fund pays no income tax on its earnings.

One of the most significant advantages of a SMSF is that there is currently no capital gains tax payable on any asset sold by a superannuation fund once its members have started to draw a pension from the fund.

## Pay off debt and purchase more land

In good years, pay off debt but not at the expense of the retirement plan. There is no point leaving a debt free farm to children when it leaves you with no money or income for retirement.

It can also be a good idea to purchase additional or different farm properties close by or geographically separate and which can become viable (but separate) units for other farming children. You may already have started doing this in your family.

## Access to aged pensions

Access to aged pensions cannot be guaranteed due to changes in government policies over time. You cannot rely on a pension and nor would you want to given how little money you would be forced to live on. This makes planning for your retirement extremely important.

Entitlement to the age pension (and other benefits) is subject to asset and income tests and for most retiring farmers, the assets will be the biggest concern.

There are three common situations that may lead to the loss of pension entitlements as they currently stand:

- **Joint Ownership of Assets**

  If investments in real estate, term deposits, shares or managed investments are held jointly with your spouse, if they die, the whole value of the assets become assessable against you.

- **Mutual Wills**

  If you have structured your will so that your assets pass to your surviving spouse, this may have a negative impact on your spouse's pension entitlements.

- **Life Insurance**

  If your surviving spouse owns the matured value of a life policy on the life of the first deceased, the surviving spouse's assets will be substantially increased and thereby impact their pension entitlements.

You cannot rely on the pension due to government policy changes and your best intentions to ensure access to the pension for your surviving spouse can actually put them in a worse financial situation. You need proper financial advice regarding your retirement strategy.[11]

*Now you've got a good idea of how much money you're going to need if you want to have a quality lifestyle when you retire. Next we will share a case study where the older generation refuses to hand over any control or assets to the next generation. After the case study, we will look at the succession planning process.*

---

11  Rural Law Online, (2014). *Farm Succession Planning: Forum Report.*

# Case Study 4:

# Dad Won't Hand Over Control or Ownership

*" If I knew I'd be in my 50s with nothing to show for all our hard work, I would have left the farm a long time ago. I am very scared for the future. We have no assets. We don't own our house or our car. We have no money for retirement. We thought we'd have control of the farm a long time ago. "*

It is often the case in family farming that a son can work for decades for a minimal wage with the promise of ownership and control at some distant point in the future that may never come. In this case, the father who is semi-retired continues to impose decisions and threatens son with removal from the farm. Meanwhile, the son and his wife are poor with no assets of their own and no funds for their impending retirement. The wife is incredibly unhappy and has been for a long time but feels trapped by age and finances.

## John & Kerrie's Story

John and Kerrie Jones run a mixed cropping and livestock farm with John's father Geoff Jones. Geoff, a widower, is semi-retired in terms of the day to day physical activities but still wields all the power in terms of decision making. He owns all the assets and he makes all the decisions and if John does something Geoff doesn't agree with, Geoff threatens to kick him off the farm.

John is now in his 50s and has worked for his dad since he was a young man, earning a basic wage. He married Kerrie in his early 20s and they have two children, Patrick and Simone. Patrick is an apprentice plumber in a local regional centre. Simone is studying finance and accounting at university.

Over the years, John and Kerrie have had a lot of fights and arguments about John continuing to work on the farm with no succession plan in place. When they were younger, Kerrie told John that they should leave the family farm because Geoff was so controlling and wouldn't allow John to make any decisions in the business. There was also a lot of tension between them because John was paid so little and if they needed a new car or improvements to their house, they had to go cap in hand begging to Geoff.

Geoff is in his 70s with no plans to hand over the reins to John and Kerrie. Whenever John and Kerrie mention succession planning, arguments happen. There have been discussions over the table from time to time but there is no plan in place. So at this stage of their lives, when they should be planning for their retirement, they have nothing.

They only argue about the farm. Kerrie wakes up in fear and worry every morning about how they are going to survive in retirement. She has lost respect for John as he hasn't stood up for their needs and has brainwashed himself into thinking that it will all work out in the end.

Their son Patrick wanted to join the family farm but Kerrie strongly encouraged him to get a trade because she is afraid that he will be put in the same situation when he has his own family.

Kerrie says, "We live like poor people. John is paid a basic wage. We don't own anything. The farm owns our house and our car. We don't own any off-farm assets. I regret not leaving the farm when I was younger but John was adamant things would work out and I trusted him."

She continues, "By the time we had children, I realised I had nowhere else to go and I felt trapped. Of course, as the children grew up, they loved living on the farm. I could leave the farm now but I have no money and even if John did come with me, he'd never forgive me for making him leave the farm.

"John believes that one day he will wake up and it will all be his and that if he leaves the farm, it will go on the market and the profits will be divided between his brothers and sisters. I have no hope for the future now. I feel like we'll be destitute when we are older."

John doesn't see things the way Kerrie does, he says, "I've put in the hard yards, I know that my dad will hand over the farm soon. He's getting old and can't work that much anymore. I've got plans to make changes on the farm as soon as I can which will increase our income and then I can give Kerrie the beach house she dreams of."

## THE LESSONS

After more than 30 years on the farm, Kerrie has felt frustrated and afraid for her future for a long time. Kerrie's advice is:

- Ask more questions
- Say what you feel and make sure everyone knows that's what you're feeling
- Stop and think, 'Is this really what I want for my life?'
- Get out early if it's not what you want
- Have a succession plan if you can – we couldn't and it's been so hard

# What is the Succession Planning Process?

# Chapter 5:

# What is the Succession Planning Process?

*"Come home son and one day this will all be yours."*

### Many a father to his son

Transitioning assets and control to younger generations has changed in recent years. The younger generation often returns to the farm after tertiary education and a career off the farm. They often return to the farm in their later 20s and early 30s. They are technologically savvy and they want to do things differently and often bring a new set of expectations of what's going to happen. And with these differing expectations, there is an even greater need for effective communication and transparency about what they can expect.

As you probably already know through personal experience or stories from friends, the succession planning process is complex and highly emotional. The planning process needs to ensure that the needs of all family members are acknowledged while ensuring a viable and sustainable farm for the future.[12]

Succession planning requires input from all the key players involved with the farm. It is rare for a succession plan to satisfy all family members 100% but certainly won't without their involvement in the planning process.

---

12  Isobel Knight | Meat & Livestock Australia (MLA) (2014). *How prepared are you? Farm business succession planning.*

## THE 6 STEPS OF SUCCESSION PLANNING

*"A great number of farmers will comment that even with all the succession planning resources available to them, they still do not know what needs to be done, by whom and in what order. Applying process, with clarity of timelines and accountability, helps in working through difficult issues.*
*The same holds true for farmers involved in succession planning. A comprehensive and integrated step-by-step approach to planning will enable farm families to work through the challenges associated with succession planning, helping to ensure that more farms are able to successfully transition ownership and management to the next generation."* [13]

Succession planning has numerous steps that need to be addressed over time. Some of these steps are not easily placed in a sequence, however, it helps to have an organised structure and methodical approach to the succession planning process.

Here's an overview of the major steps in developing a succession plan:

- Step 1: **Communication** & Discussion

- Step 2: Collect & Analyse **Information**

- Step 3: Generate & Assess **Options**

- Step 4: Make Preliminary **Decisions**

- Step 5: **Design**, Develop, Write & Review

- Step 6: **Implement**, Monitor & Review

*Please understand that these steps are not necessarily completed one after the other. Some may be done one after the other, some done at the same time, and others in random order.*

---

13  Fleming Muntz Solicitors (2008). *Succession and Estate Planning for Country Clients.*

## Step 1: Communication & Discussion

This step is often the hardest but you need to open the lines of communication about succession planning and put it openly on the agenda for the whole family. First, start the conversation, then work out what everyone wants and then see how they all fit together.

**Start the Conversation & Open the Lines of Communication**

This is the most important first step in the succession planning process. You need to open the lines of communication between the generations and among all involved family members. Once the family starts talking, you can all think about your involvement in the future of the farm.

Good communication skills help any business perform better. Connecting with your family members and workers in a respectful and constructive manner is essential in developing your succession plan.

Remember, though, that communication is more than just talking. Sometimes you need to be quiet and listen. Really listen to what the other person is saying and let them know that you hear them. This is part of the key to negotiating a succession plan. Most people really want to be heard and have their needs taken into account.

You might think it's a bit too formal having a written communications plan but it can really help you during the succession planning process.

See *Chapter 6: What's in a Succession Plan?* for more details about your communications plan.

**Define Personal, Family and Business Objectives and Goals**

Once your family has opened the lines of communication about succession planning, the next step is for each party to define their separate objectives, goals and expectations for themselves, their family and the business.

The key objectives to focus on for succession planning are:

- Improving operational integrity and efficiencies

- Enhancing financial security for each family unit
- Providing opportunities for work-life balance
- Preparing the next generation to lead the operation

**Identify Successors**

If you are the successor generation, one of the key considerations in defining objectives and goals is being really honest about whether you want to be involved in the family farming business or not. If you do, you become a potential successor and the succession process then moves forward in transitioning to the next generation.

If you don't want to be involved in the farming business, then discussions and decisions need to be about preserving family wealth and transitioning out of farming.

**Assessment of Compatibility of Objectives and Goals**

Once a successor has been identified, you need to honestly assess the compatibility of everyone's business and personal objectives, goals and expectations.

There are a number of different factors that affect each person's objectives, goals and expectations. These include past family history, family values, personality conflicts, family relationship dynamics, favouritism, life stages issues and associated challenges.[14]

If there are serious incompatibilities, then you are in trouble and you need to develop a strategy to address these. You may also need an outside facilitator to assist you with this.

The main goal here is to reach a consensus on the major objectives and goals. You can't really move forward in the succession planning process until there is a level of agreement among the different parties.

---

14 Ontario Ministry of Agriculture, Food & Rural Affairs (OMAFRA). *Components of a Farm Succession Plan.*

## Step 2: Collect & Analyse Information

In this step, information is gathered and analysed in order to:

- Improve the farming family's general knowledge of succession planning
- Collect relevant technical information (particularly financial)
- Analyse financial viability and profitability of the farm business
- Review additional specific technical information

### Get a Basic Understanding of Succession Planning

Everyone involved in the succession planning process needs to have some idea of the process. You can educate yourself by reading articles, going to a seminar or workshop or just reading this book. If everyone involved read this book, you would all start on the same page and hopefully get through the whole process more quickly and easily.

### Collect Relevant Technical Information

Next, pull together relevant technical information about the farm. Compile and review the legal will, the power of attorney, tax returns, financial statements, current financing arrangements, retirement savings position and any business and legal agreements, etc. Identify any missing pieces. This is a prerequisite to completing an analysis of the farm business's financial situation to determine viability and profitability.

Some of the technical information you need to collect includes:

- Legal will(s)
- Power(s) of attorney
- Property deeds
- Mortgages and loan information
- Past and any current tax records and information
- Past and current financial records

- Past and current financial statements

- Past and current production and performance records

- Bank account information

- Savings and off-farm investment information

- Retirement planning and savings

- A current list of debts and other liabilities

- A current list of suppliers and service providers (e.g. lawyer, accountant, nutritionist/feed company, equipment supplier, etc.)

- Any other business related material or information

If you're looking at this list thinking that's a lot of information to collect, you are right. But this is the information you need to have organised, regardless of succession planning, as part of managing your business.

**Document Assets & Liabilities**

You also need to need to gather the following information as part of the succession planning process:

- **Land Ownership**
    - Title references
    - Acreages
    - Relative location of properties
    - Mortgagees

- **Plant & Livestock**
    - Numbers
    - Breeding stock
    - Artificial insemination strategies
    - Other relevant information

- **Structures of the Family Enterprise**
    - Any companies, trusts, partnerships, super funds etc.

- **Improvements**

  Description of improvements made and their location (this is important if the farm is to be divided between children). For example, if the farm was to be divided between two sons and one block had a machinery shed and silos and the other did not, there would be an inequity.

- **Documentation**

  Copies of all relevant documents including trust deeds, partnership agreements, company returns, insurance policies, super fund, etc.

- **Financial Statements**

  Analysis and report on financial statements to ascertain the viability of the farming enterprise and to understand the current debt level.

- **Other Assets**

  Copies of all farm management deposits (FMDs), shares, off-farm real estate, etc. and a list of who owns what.

### Analyse Financial Viability and Profitability of the Farm Business

Once the financial information is collected, use the financial statements to analyse the farm business's past and current financial situation.

The farm's financial performance can then be compared to industry benchmarks to determine the farm's relative current financial situation and profitability. In addition, develop projected cash flow and income statements to investigate the potential future financial situation and viability of the business.

The business has to be profitable and viable. If it does not currently generate enough income, what changes can be made to ensure it does in the near future?

The question is, "Does the business currently generate enough income (i.e. profit) to support another household, provide for a financially secure retirement for the founders and ensure a financially sound business for the successor(s)?

Family living costs are a serious consideration at this time. Review whether there will be any drastic changes in family living requirements over the next while (e.g. a family member active in the business getting married, having children, building a house, etc.).

### Review Additional Specific Technical Information

Consider any additional relevant specific technical information. This includes details related to methods of transfer, financing options, tax and legal considerations, business structures and such. This information is helpful in the next step where you generate different options for going forward.

## Step 3: Generate & Assess Options

When you've got an understanding of the business' assets and liabilities and the needs and wishes of stakeholders, it is time to have a look at options for the future.

These options need to address the various issues related to but not limited to:

- Ownership **transfer** options-purchase, rent, gifts, bequests, etc.

- **Financing** options (both internal and external)

- Business **organisations/structures** (i.e. sole proprietorship, partnership, corporation, etc.)

- **Legal** considerations (e.g. will, power of attorney, etc.); inclusion of dispute resolution mechanisms in business agreements

- **Tax** strategies and implications

Investigate different "what if" scenarios and develop contingencies to address the 5 Ds (disagreement, disaster, death, disability and divorce). Flexibility is the key. You may want to get a good facilitator to help your family review the various options. (For more information, see *Chapter 8: Do you need Professional Help?)*

When you have a good list of options, assess each to test the strength of the option for the long-term health of the farming business. Here are some criteria you can use to assess your options:

- How does the option impact the overall **financial viability** of the farm?

- How does the option fit with each **stakeholder's goals** and needs?
- How **realistic** is this option – can it be achieved?
- Does the option allow for the current **owner's wishes** and retirement plans?
- Who won't be **happy** with option?

## Step 4: Make Preliminary Decisions

This is where you make some preliminary decisions about the general direction of the succession plan and then focus on the individual preferences, needs and expectations. This is where you would call in a team of advisors to help you investigate your options (see *Chapter 8: Do you need Professional Help?*).

Once your family has a good idea about how you want to proceed, what you want to achieve and in what timeframe, you can create a rough plan.

## Step 5: Design, Develop, Write and Review

Phew, getting to this stage is pretty tough going. You've collected a ton of information, talked your heads off, and now hopefully, there's a sense of agreement about how you are going to proceed. Step 5 is where all the details get nutted out and where you have to make some decisions.

In your written succession plan, you basically describe what your family wants to happen with your farm business.

Your plan can include the following:

1. Executive Summary

2. Business Overview

3. Strategic Plan

4. Retirement Plan

5. Management, Control and Labour Transfer Plan

6. Ownership Transfer Plan

7. Financial Plan

8. Action Plan & Implementation Timetable

9. Supporting Documents

10. Training and Development Plan for Successor

11. Communications Plan

12. Contingency Plan

(To find out more about what you need to include in your succession plan, see *Chapter 6: What's in a Succession Plan?*)

At this stage, things may come up that send you back to the drawing board. You may need to generate new options or change something. This is perfectly normal, so don't worry if this happens during this step. And don't forget, it's really important that everyone is comfortable with what's going on, so if that means looking at a different option, go for it.

As decisions are documented, call on your team of advisors to review the plan and provide detailed feedback, advice and comments.

Once you have a good draft ready, you need to conduct a review and have a discussion with all parties. This should be an open and transparent process. After this, you can make any changes needed to the plan before you go ahead and implement it.

*Don't forget your plan needs to be practical and straight forward so that it can actually be implemented rather than stay in a filing cabinet or on your computer.*

## Step 6: Implement, Monitor & Review

You've come a long way in the process and you're finally up to implementing your succession plan. Give each family member a copy of the plan and create an atmosphere of openness and shared responsibility. This helps reduce concerns and possible misunderstandings as the plan unfolds. The timetable should be followed and monitored. Make sure that everyone knows what they're responsible for and that they actually do it.

It's normal for issues to arise but you need to be on top of them and modify the plan as needed. Flexibility is the key here. If something needs to be changed or adjusted, then follow through with the appropriate action.

And finally, don't forget to celebrate your success. Creating and implementing a succession plan is huge! Throw yourself a succession party if you want. This is big stuff. And it will make a huge difference to the whole family now that it is sorted!

## SUCCESSFUL SUCCESSION PLANNING

A good succession plan is where everyone has a clear understanding of what's going to happen over the next 5 to 10 years and they feel that most of their needs and desires have been taken into account.

People might not get everything they want on their wish list but if there has been enough communication and they have an understanding of why things are being done the way they are, they are more likely to be satisfied with the outcome.

Succession planning also has to include a mechanism for responding to the changing circumstances of those involved in the farming business, whether it's death, illness, injury/disability, changes in marital status (marriage or divorce), having children or not wanting to farm anymore.

Remember, a succession plan needs to be a ***Living Document.*** It's not something you create once, throw in a filing cabinet or drawer and then forget about.

You can think of succession planning as a relay race.[15] Success depends on these four things:

- **Sequence**

    Prepare the successor with the leadership skills and business experience to lead the operation. Prepare the operation and the current owner for a seamless transition.

- **Timing**

    Incrementally pass the torch of leadership from one generation to the next over the course of a predetermined period of time.

---

15  AgWeb - Farm Journal Legacy Project, (2014). *Legacy Workbook.*

- **Baton Passing**

  Manage the business and familial details of the process for a smooth and seamless transition.

- **Communication**

  Ensure an information exchange between the senior generation and successor(s). In many cases, owners choose to communicate with active and inactive family members as well.

## Speed Humps/Road Blocks

There may be a number of speed humps or road blocks that slow down or stall the succession planning process. These might come up in regard to educating children (e.g. boarding school or getting a second base in a city or regional centre) and a sense of inequity if one sibling doesn't have children.

Early in the succession planning process, confront and consider the following common obstacles:

- Who are the **right successors**, whether family or non-family members?

- How is the **financial security** of the primary owner/s going to be ensured?

- What is a **workable** transition of ownership?

- Who are the **extended stakeholders** and how can they be involved (loyal employees, alliance partners and family)?

## How to Kill a Succession Plan

Sometimes a succession plan is doomed from the beginning. This can be especially true if the starting point is not right – if you leave it too late and things are already in trouble.

Here are a couple of ways to kill a succession plan:

- Start when things are already in bad shape – sometimes it's too little too late!

- Give away or keep control of assets not actually owned by the person giving them away (this can easily happen as assets are often sitting in different entities due to taxation).

*Now you've got an understanding of the whole succession planning process. Next we will share a case study where the father remarries and then leaves everything to his new wife. After the case study, we will have a look at what is actually in a succession plan.*

# Case Study 5:

# Dad Remarries & Leaves Everything to His New Wife

*" I was happy for Dad when he found someone to share his life with. He missed Mum terribly and I just wanted to see him smile. I didn't realise that when he died, his new wife would get everything my brother and I had worked for. "*

When the father and owner of the family farm gets a new spouse, things can quickly change for the younger generation, especially if they pass away before their new spouse and no official plans are in place or an updated will.

## Pete's Story

My dad, Calvin Jones, was happily married to Irma for more than 35 years. When she passed away suddenly at aged 60 from breast cancer, Calvin was bereft. He felt like he was missing a limb. At first, he was very withdrawn and had a hard time socialising. Eventually, at the urging of my siblings and me, he took up bowls at the local club, where he met a woman called Gina who had lost her husband a few years earlier.

Calvin and Gina started dating, much to the horror of her children and my siblings. We felt like they were too old for romance and were acting like teenagers. But Calvin and Gina adored each other and didn't want to spend the rest of their lives alone. They knew that life was precious and didn't want to waste it worrying about what other people thought, even their kids.

Gina and Calvin got married relatively quickly as they didn't see the point in delaying, given their age. The new family dynamics were tense. Gina had three children, one son and two daughters.

My dad didn't have a succession plan in place and we didn't think much about it. My brother Ross and I worked on the farm thinking we would inherit the farm together when our father died. My sister, Jenny, has been told that she would inherit the house in town that our mother owned prior to her death and was willed to dad.

One day out of the blue, Dad complained about feeling ill and was rushed to hospital where he had a massive stroke and died. We were devastated, as was Gina. What none of us knew, even Gina, was that Calvin had no will. Gina inherited everything. Ross, Jenny and I were in shock as we sat in the office of our family lawyer.

Ross and I had spent a lifetime working the farm with Dad and now he was dead and his wife of less than two years inherited everything. Gina decided to keep everything because she was legally entitled to it and she knew it would then go to her children and set them up for life. She moved into the investment house in town and started trying to sell the farm.

All of a sudden, my brother and I and our families had nowhere to live and no income. Ross, Jenny and I launched a legal dispute to claim what was rightfully ours. It was a costly exercise and took a long time and everyone involved was stressed and unhappy. While the courts did favour us in the end, it took more than a year to resolve and we still had to give Gina quite a lot of money.

## THE LESSONS

- You never know when things are going to change and they can do so very quickly

- You need to have official plans and documents in place to protect your future

- Make sure your estate planning is up to date and reflects changes in circumstances

- Have a succession plan in place that ensures transition of assets and control

- Make sure you have life insurance

# What's in a Succession Plan?

# Chapter 6:

# What's in a Succession Plan?

*" Succession planning is a continuous process to plan for the transfer of knowledge, skills, labour, management, control and ownership of the farm business between one generation, sometimes known as the founder or retiring generation, and the next or successor generation. Succession is a process and not an event; it takes time and effort to work through and develop a comprehensive plan that best meets the needs of the farm family. "* [16]

By now, you've got a pretty good idea of what succession planning is all about. Your written farm succession plan records and describes the decisions made about how the transfer of the knowledge, skills, labour, control, management and ownership will occur and when.

There are a lot of necessary components that make up a sound succession plan. It can seem overwhelming when you look at the list but don't be put off. The components of your succession plan are really important and many of them are valuable, separately from the succession plan, in how you run your business.

So, here are the common components of a Farm Succession Plan:

1. Executive Summary
2. Business Overview
3. Strategic Plan
4. Retirement Plan
5. Management, Control & Labour Transfer Plan
6. Ownership Transfer Plan

---

16  Ontario Ministry of Agriculture, Food & Rural Affairs (OMAFRA). *Components of a Farm Succession Plan.*

7. Financial Plan
8. Action Plan & Implementation Timetable
9. Supporting Documents
10. Training & Development Plan for Successor
11. Communications Plan
12. Contingency Plan

*Are you thinking, "OMG! I didn't realise a succession plan was made up of so many other plans!"*

This list may look daunting right now as it has so many different elements but all these different components need to fit together to create an integrated and comprehensive plan. Let's take a look at the different components that make up a succession plan.

## 1. EXECUTIVE SUMMARY

The summary provides a quick scan of the plan without having to read the full document. Generally written after the succession plan has been drafted, the executive summary summarises the plan and includes an overview of the current business, goals, strategies, action points and the timeline to implement the plan. Even though it's the first thing in your plan, write this last.

## 2. BUSINESS OVERVIEW

This sets the stage for the rest of the plan and provides a clear and concise picture of the business. Similar to a business plan, it is useful to begin with an overview of the business that everyone involved understands and agrees upon.

This may include things like:

- The size and location of your farming operation
- What the farm produces and how much
- Who's involved in the business and in what capacity (decision making, header driving, shearing, cropping, etc.)
- The type of business structure and other arrangements that are in place (such as sole proprietor, corporation, partnership, rental agreements, etc.)

## 3. STRATEGIC PLAN

The strategic plan is the starting point for really getting to the heart of your succession plan. It describes the short and long term business and personal goals and expectations of the retiring generation and the next generations.

It details the various strategies that need to be implemented to meet these goals.

In strategic planning, you need to discuss, clarify, address and define these goals and expectations and write them down. This helps ensure that everyone has a clear understanding of the strategic plan for the farming operations.

Once completed, the rest of the process and the resulting plan flow from it.

## 4. RETIREMENT PLAN

It's very important to have a retirement plan (or as we like to call it, a harvest strategy). You want to be able to enjoy your retirement. Creating a retirement plan involves two core issues – lifestyle and finances. Basically, it's about what sort of life you want to have when you're retired and how you plan to pay for it.

Lifestyle considerations include what sort of activities you want to be involved in when you're retired, how involved you will be in the business and where you will live.

Financial considerations include where the money will come from (e.g. sale of farm, interest, savings, etc.) as well as any income generating strategies and expected cost of living.

## 5. MANAGEMENT, CONTROL & LABOUR TRANSFER PLAN

The transfer plan describes how the transfer of management, control and labour (basically decision-making and workload) to the successor will take place. It also includes a timetable for this transition.

The successors need to have the competence to manage the business before full responsibility is transferred to them. This might mean they need to have training to ensure they have the skills and knowledge to run the business and why you may also need to have a training and development plan for the successor/s.

## 6. OWNERSHIP TRANSFER PLAN

The ownership transfer plan describes the current business structure and outlines how it will change during the transfer process. It should include a description of the intended business arrangement (e.g. sole proprietorship, partnership, corporation, etc.).

The ownership transfer plan includes:[17]

- An explanation of the **financing** required, the various sources available and the preferred financing option(s)

- An **inventory** and **valuation** of assets and liabilities

- An explanation of the **tax implications** of the proposed transfer process along with a description of how these items will be addressed

- A discussion regarding the treatment of **non-farming children**

- An outline of the **insurance** requirements related to life, disability, disaster and related insurance tools

- A description of the **legal agreements** (e.g. employment contracts, partnership agreements, shareholder agreements, buy-sell agreements, etc.).

Copies of these should be attached as appendices to your succession plan for reference purposes. It should be ensured that these legal agreements include dispute resolution mechanisms. You also need to keep copies of wills and prenuptial agreements in the appendices as well.

## 7. FINANCIAL PLAN

The financial plan describes how the farm business will meet the needs of the retirees and successors. It includes a financial analysis of the farm business - past, present and future - to determine if the business is profitable and viable.

This is critical because if the business is not currently profitable and viable, then strategies need to be identified to make it so. The financial plan also outlines the future direction of the farm business (for example, expansion,

---

17 PNC Bank (2011). *Succession Planning on the Farm.*

diversification, downsizing etc.) and how this direction will affect the business and projected financials.

## 8. ACTION PLAN & IMPLEMENTATION TIMETABLE

The action plan and implementation timetable list the key activities that need to be implemented and by when. Key activities need to be prioritised with deadlines so that you can monitor and measure your progress. This will also help you work out what you might need to change or amend as you are going along.

## 9. SUPPORTING DOCUMENTS

There's a truck load of business, legal and financial documents that you need as part of your succession plan. You need to put copies of each of the necessary documents into this section of your plan so that they are easily accessible and all in one place.

## 10. TRAINING & DEVELOPMENT PLAN FOR SUCCESSOR

As discussed above, before the transfer of decision making and ownership, it's critical that the next generation has the skills and knowledge to successfully run the farming operations. Given the complexity of farming these days, this is even more important than ever.

A training and development plan outlines the skills and knowledge required by the successor and compares these with the current skills ("skills profile") of the successor. Any gaps can be identified and an action plan can be developed to address these gaps.

## 11. COMMUNICATIONS PLAN

We don't need to tell you that communication is your key to creating a succession plan that really meets the needs of everyone involved so a communications plan can be a really useful part of part of your succession plan.

Your communication plan might have these two components:

1.  A description of how your family is going to communicate regarding succession planning and transition

2.   A discussion about how your family will manage and resolve disputes

## Communicating about Succession Planning

*   Schedule **regular** "family business" meetings

*   Outline who **participates** in these meetings (e.g. Is it for only those active in the farm business or can all family members attend?)

*   If the meetings are only for those active in the business, decide whether you need a separate "family" meeting for all family members

*   Decide **where** to meet and if meals will be involved

*   Outline **responsibilities and decision-making process** (e.g. Who will set up the meeting and agenda, follow-up on decisions, chair the meetings, etc.?)

*   Create some **ground rules** and make sure everyone is aware of them (e.g. Everyone has a turn to talk, don't interrupt the person speaking, no blaming, stay focussed on the agenda item, etc.)

*   Write up and distribute written **agendas** ahead of the meeting

*   Record the meeting or have someone take **minutes**

*   Outline the **dispute process** as agreed upon as per the following section

## Managing Disputes

As you know, there will be times when people just won't agree on things. So it can be really helpful to have a discussion – before a dispute arises – about how you are going to deal with disputes.

You may decide that each member of the family gets to vote on the issue or that a third-party mediator needs to be called in. Whatever you decide, it's important that you have this discussion ahead of time.

You don't want to be arguing about how you're going to manage a dispute while you're already in the middle of one.

## 12. CONTINGENCY PLAN

Every succession plan needs to address the 5Ds:

- Death

- Disability

- Disease

- Divorce

- Disagreements

You just never know when something is going to change and you want to have a contingency plan in place to help you sort things out in what would already be a stressful enough time.

In your contingency plan, you can refer to insurance requirements, including life, disability and disaster insurance, as key components of your contingency plan and risk management.

*So now you know what to include in your succession plan – yes, there are a lot of documents, but don't let that put you off. Next we will share a case study where the father dies after a long partnership and things were not handled well. After the case study, we will have a quick look at estate planning and how it differs from succession planning.*

# Case Study 6:

# Father Dies After a Long Partnership with Son

*" After a lifetime of working with my father, with a partnership agreement in place and the assurance that the farm would be mine, I had to fight tooth and nail to get what was mine. It cost me a lot of money and ruined my relationship with my siblings. "*

Sometimes you think that everything is sorted. You will inherit as promised. You have a partnership agreement in place. Then you find out that your parent's will takes that all away from you.

### Jack's Story

Jack O'Brian had been farming with his father for more than 30 years. His father repeatedly told Jack that the farm would be his. They already had a written partnership agreement that made Jack an equal partner in the farm business, which included the land purchased by the partnership, but Jack's dad held all the documents and financial records and paid Jack a wage.

For his whole adult life, Jack had worked on his father's farm for a basic wage. His father was an older man in ill health, which had meant that Jack was the main labourer and decision maker.

Jack had assisted in building up the farm assets, partnership assets and the capital improvements on the land owned by his father. Although he was an equal partner in the farming business, he was not involved in the financial management on a day to day basis.

Upon the death of Jack's father, Jack was surprised to find out that his father's will provided for the distribution of farm assets between Jack's mother and siblings. This included partnership assets instead of the partnership share.

Jack was forced to challenge the will and it took a long time for the court to rule on the case. In the meantime, the value of the land increased considerably. This meant that he had to buy back "his" farm at market value, giving him less than 60% equity and less than 75% of the original farm. For all his years of hard work, he was basically treated the same as his off-farm siblings.

As a result of all of this, Jack's relationship with his family is strained. In challenging the will, he created a rift in his family, but at his age he needed to take care of his own financial future so that he and his wife could eventually retire themselves.

## THE LESSONS

- Fairness and equality are not the same thing – in this case, the farming son was treated very unfairly in being treated equally with his off-farm siblings

- If you are in partnership, you need to have access to the financial statements for the business

- If you are in partnership, make sure you have a signed copy of the partnership agreement

- Proper estate planning should be in place to protect farming partners upon your death

- Consider setting up a trust to provide for the on-farm child who has worked on the farm for most of their adult life

- Instead of getting paid a full wage, purchase the land from the father via vendor loan

# Chapter 7

# What about Estate Planning?

# Chapter 7:

# What about Estate Planning?

*"Death comes to all, but great achievements
build a monument which shall endure until
the sun grows cold."*

Ralph Waldo Emerson

## DIFFERENCE BETWEEN SUCCESSION PLANNING & ESTATE PLANNING

Many people are confused about the difference between succession planning and estate planning. These two are not the same! They are both important and they both interact with each other and have elements that need to be resolved and become part of the overall plan to transition ownership and management to the next generations.

Estate planning is about **anticipating and arranging the disposal of assets**, and it includes wills, insurance and other legal documents.

Succession planning is about the **transfer of control of decision making and assets**.

There are two main aims of estate planning:

1.  To try and avoid the likelihood of any next of kin suffering financially and

2.  To minimise the risk of family disagreements about who gets what.

Estate planning can help you ensure that your estate is passed on to your beneficiaries in the most financially efficient and tax effective way possible.

An estate plan needs to:

- Be simple to administer
- Not be too expensive to manage
- Balance the life-time enjoyment of assets and income while preserving assets for the family after death
- Be reviewed regularly

# ESTATE PLANNING ESSENTIALS

Estate planning and succession planning really go hand in hand. A succession plan can never work if there's no estate plan.

So what sort of things do you need to have in place as part of your estate plan?

- Will
- Testamentary Trusts
- Power of Attorney
- Living Will/Power of Attorney for Healthcare

## Will

A will is an important document that all members of the family should have once they are over 18 years old. A will can only deal with personally held assets though. Any assets held by companies or family trusts cannot be included as they are held by another entity. Family trusts, (discretionary trusts) have been used in agriculture for many years as a liability protection mechanism and for tax mitigation.

## Testamentary Trusts

A testamentary trust is a discretionary trust created within a will that only comes into effect upon the death of the person making the will.

Basically, a trust is a where assets are managed by one person (known as the trustee) for the benefits of others (beneficiary/beneficiaries).

If you have dependent children, in particular, you might want to have a testamentary trust as part of your will because it allows for greater flexibility in distributing assets as well as greater asset protection and potential taxation reducing benefits.

## Power of Attorney

An important part of estate planning is having a documented power of attorney.

A power of attorney gives the person you designate as your power of attorney the right to act on your behalf if you lose your capacity to make decisions due to an accident, ill health or ageing.

A will only takes effect on death, whereas a power of attorney gives power to another to control his or her affairs during their lifetime with the use of a "power of attorney".

If a person loses their capacity to make decisions and they have no power of attorney, the consequences can be quite dramatic and traumatic for their family. Assets may be frozen, joint assets will be hard to manage and a whole lot of legal processes would become necessary to manage the assets.

It's a nightmare that can be avoided by assigning a power of attorney. But don't worry, the power of attorney can be revoked and changed at any time which means you can choose someone to be your power of attorney now but if your relationship changes, you can always choose someone else.

In a farming business, every equity owner really needs to have at least a financial power of attorney, so that the business can continue to operate uninterrupted despite accident or illness.

## A Living Will or Power of Attorney for Healthcare

A living will is a legal document where you can specify what actions should be taken with regards to your health should you become unable to make decisions for yourself if you are ill or injured.

A living will allows you to be very clear about what sort of treatment and care you would like if you become unable to make medical decisions for yourself.

You can appoint a power of attorney to make medical decisions on your behalf. If you have specific ideas about what you do and don't want done, you can document them, as well as discuss them with the person you have chosen as your power of attorney in the event of your incapacitation.

## Beneficiary Forms

Get organised with your superannuation, bank accounts and life insurance policies by assigning beneficiaries who would receive your funds upon your death. This can really save a lot of time and energy in the long run but can be annoying for you as you have to contact each financial institution and get a beneficiary form which you complete and then return to them.

# WARNING: A WILL IS NOT A SUCCESSION PLAN!

*"A will is not a succession plan!"*

## Nick Shady

A final note on estate planning – please do not use your will as a succession tool!

Here are some good reasons why you can't rely on your will as a replacement for a succession plan:

- After you're dead, family members can challenge your will and have it overturned.

- Challenges to wills are expensive and usually split families.

- If your will is not up to date and does not have all your assets listed on it, there may be trouble.

- A succession plan is a living document that needs to change and be revised as part of an ongoing process that involves the whole family. It's unlikely that you will want to change your will regularly and amending wills can also be expensive.

- If there are issues around equity and fairness, these are better addressed through a succession plan (and before there is a death in the family).

- A will does not provide the same structure as a succession plan and is limited as a succession planning tool.

- You can only leave in your will what you own at the time of death. Your will cannot take into account assets held in a discretionary trust.

---

*If you don't have a current will, you should make it a priority. Now it's time to have a look at a case study where both parents die suddenly without a will and the mess that created for the family. After the case study, we will have a chat about the need for professional help and how to go about gathering the right team.*

---

## Case Study 7:

# Both Parents Die Suddenly Without a Will

*" I didn't realise my parents never made a will. I just assumed they did. By not having a will, the farm was split equally among the three children. I was lucky because my brothers knew that the farm should go to me and they gave me their share. If it wasn't for their generosity and understanding, I wouldn't be farming today."*

Failing to have a sound estate in place is just asking for trouble. Even if you haven't got a succession plan in place, get a will drawn up this week. You leave your family in a vulnerable position if you don't because your assets will be divvied up according to state law. When someone dies "intestate" – without a will – state laws apply.

### Robert's Story

For more than ten years, I had farmed with my father. We never really spoke about succession planning but I assumed that I would inherit the farm and my two younger brothers who had no interest in farming, would inherit Mum and Dad's shares and cash deposits.

One day, I got a phone call from the local police officer. Both my parents had been killed in a freak car accident. We were all shocked by the suddenness of their deaths. We had never thought of losing our parents because they were so young, let alone losing both of them at the same time.

I didn't realise that Mum and Dad never had a will drawn up and because they died without a will, the three of us inherited equal shares in the farm under state law. I was devastated. The farm couldn't provide for all three of us and my brothers weren't interested in farming anyway.

Thankfully, my brothers acknowledged that they had their education paid for by the farm and that I had sacrificed a lot to stay on the farm and earn a pitiful salary. My brothers met behind my back and discussed the situation.

They decided that the fairest thing was for me to own the farm and they would keep any other assets. To this day, I am so thankful for them. I know that I couldn't have carried on farming if it wasn't for their generosity.

I know a few other families who were in a similar position but their situation didn't turn out very well. Some families don't even speak to each other anymore because of this type of situation. I've seen it more when the siblings are already married and more than one is working the farm.

## THE LESSONS

- Tragedy can happen at any time – your life can change in just one second
- Start succession planning now
- Regardless of where you are in the succession planning process, make sure you have a valid and up-to-date will
- Don't let money come between family members – people are more important than anything else
- If you die without a will, the relevant laws will determine how your assets are distributed
- Life insurance for working partners is important
- Purchase some land from the parents at market value to create some capital in the future

# Do you need Professional Help?

# Chapter 8:

# Do you need Professional Help?

*" With so much on the line - generations of wealth, relationships, whole businesses – it is crucial to get succession planning right. It takes a lot of expertise to develop a succession plan that involves estate planning, accounting, legal advice and possibly conciliation. "*

### Ayesha Hilton

Succession planning is complex. It's emotional. And it involves your future. So, you will definitely need professionals to help you navigate the various financial, legal and emotional road blocks along the way.

By now, you've got a good idea of how much work is involved in creating a good succession plan. You've got to gather information, analyse it, discuss it and make decisions - all with family members with potentially different needs and expectations. No wonder so many farming families don't have a formal succession plan.

So, if you're feeling a little overwhelmed at the thought of creating your succession plan, don't bail out now. You can get help that will make a big difference to the whole experience as well as the outcome.

To develop and implement your plan and to guide you along the way, you need a team of professional advisors. They can help you answer key questions about the future of your farm and help you create a succession plan that your family can all feel happy with.

Here are some of the professionals that can assist in your succession planning process:

- **Accountant** to help you determine your current position and structures, taxation minimisation strategies and the best structure of the business now and in the future.

- **Succession Planning Consultant** to facilitate the succession planning process and guide you and your family through the succession planning maze.

- **Facilitator/Moderator** to facilitate family discussions and to hold the vision for the future as you go through the succession planning process (if you have a succession planning consultant, they would act as facilitator).

- **Financial/Estate Planner** to help evaluate retirement, investment and superannuation options.

- **Farm Management Consultant** to help you assess the potential of your farming operation or advice on new market opportunities.

- **Solicitor** to help you with the estate planning, wills, tax matters and other legal issues as well as advising on what is legal and what is not.

- **Insurance Agent** to help you work out the appropriate insurance for family members to ensure that everyone has coverage in case of death or disability.

- **Registered Valuer** to help you work out the value of your real estate and other farm assets.

- Your **Bank Manager** or lender who will not only be literally doing a happy dance because you are undertaking succession planning but will also be able to work with you if you are planning to expand the farming operation.

*Don't be 'penny wise, pound foolish.' Make sure you get good professional advice.*

## SHOULD YOU USE A SPECIALIST SUCCESSION PLANNING CONSULTANT?

Succession planning is a complex undertaking at the best of times but if there are family misunderstandings and potential for conflict, get professional help from a succession planning consultant.

The advantage of using a succession planning consultant is that they are trained to be unbiased and to mediate in difficult emotional situations and assist with the 'process' rather than just acting as an 'advisor'.

If the writing is on the wall and you already know there's going to be a lot of conflict during the succession planning process, you really should consider enlisting a succession planning consultant. They can help your family reach a general agreement on a succession plan.

There are a number of companies who specialise in succession planning (please see our resource guide for more information).

## The Pros

Here are some of the benefits of using a specialist succession planner:

- Specialised expertise in succession planning
- Experienced in different succession planning models
- Understanding of the specific challenges involved in succession planning
- Conciliation and mediation skills to assist in resolving conflict
- Assisting in the coordination of the other professional advisors
- Provides independence, objectivity and control

## The Cons

There are a lot of reasons for using a succession planning specialist but you also need to be aware that they may not have deep level knowledge of financial planning, legal issues, estate planning, taxation and mediation – you will still need specialist advice on these issues.

## What can you expect from a succession planning consultant?

This really depends on the succession planning consultant you hire and what level of involvement you want from them. Most succession planning consultants or companies provide different packages depending on how involved you want them to be in your succession planning process.

They can help you assess your readiness for succession planning, develop your plan with all members of the family farm business, implement the plan and then review and amend it as necessary.

When you schedule your succession planning meetings, it's best to meet somewhere neutral, off-farm, where there are no distractions. Make the environment feel safe and comfortable. Organise catering if needed. All the different stakeholders and those impacted by the decisions need to attend the meeting. This includes in-laws and long-term partners as well as workers.

**Creating Your Own Team of Experts**

*" Coming together is a beginning. Keeping together is progress. Working together is success. "*

Henry Ford

A professional succession planning team makes all the difference. Creating a team of experts is an important part of your succession planning process. You need a team of advisors that you trust and feel comfortable with. You want to feel like you can talk to them and that they understand where you're coming from.

If you already have a financial planner, a solicitor and an accountant, just make sure that you are comfortable with them and if not, shop around for the right people. You don't have to settle for the ones you've got, just because you have been with them for what feels like forever.

## How to Choose Your Experts

In choosing your team of expert advisors, here is what you need to look for:

- Up-to-date knowledge and expertise in their field
- A willingness to communicate openly with family members
- An ability to explain technical terms in easy to understand language
- An understanding of family dynamics, especially in farming families
- A willingness to work in collaboration with other advisors
- Happy to ask the hard questions
- Ability to be honest even when it's difficult for the clients to hear
- Has current indemnity insurance

## How to Interview Potential Experts

When choosing new advisors, you can set up an appointment with them and basically interview them to see if they are a good fit for you and your family.

Here are some examples of questions you could ask them:[18]

- What kind of training do you have?

- What certification do you have (Law, Accounting, AgriBusiness, Financial Planning Accreditation, etc.)?

- How long have you been doing this kind of work?

- What experience do you have in working with farm businesses similar to ours?

- What farm succession planning experience do you have?

- How much are your fees and what is the fee structure?

- Give them some example situations and ask them how they would approach these situations.

- Ask for references and check with them.

It is really important that you feel comfortable with your advisors as you will be working with them closely on quite personal and emotional stuff, so make sure they are a right fit for you!

As you can see, there are a lot of different advisors that you will call upon during the succession planning process. Choosing a team of highly skilled and knowledgeable advisors will help you develop and implement a sound succession plan. And hopefully make the whole process easier for everyone!

*Now you know what professionals you need on your team and trust us, having a team of professionals makes the whole process so much easier. Next we will share a case study about a farmer with no children and what he did to create a legacy. After the case study, we will look at strategies you can put in place to minimise conflict during the succession planning process.*

---

18  GRDC, Judy Wilkinson & Lyn Sykes (2007). *A GUIDE TO SUCCESSION Sustaining Families and Farms.*

# Case Study 8:

# No Children to Leave the Farm To

*" You've got to realise it's not all take, you've got to give. Handing over is so important. I'm pretty pig-headed, I didn't think I'd ever handover but I've really found myself enjoy handing over and watching the success of the next generation," says Ray Harrington from Darkan in Western Australia, who, with no sons of his own, teamed up with his nephew Tim to plot a path for the future."* [19]

There are a number of bachelor farmers who have never gotten married. These men work hard on their farm creating a legacy and they want to share this legacy with someone, often an extended family member. If done right, this can create an opportunity where the family member would never have to work or own a piece of farming property and it gives the original farm owner the chance to work with the younger generation, expand their operation and remain on the farm longer.

## Graham & James' Story

Graham Molloy was working his 5,000 hectare grain and livestock farm alone for many years with only help from casual employees as needed. With no sons of his own, and needing additional help on his farm, he needed help. But he only wanted to work with family. Graham's older brother, Shane, had four sons all working on his farm.

Graham chose his youngest nephew, James, to work with him. James agreed. The arrangement was that James would work for Graham for 10 years for a minimal wage and after 10 years, James would get half of the farm.

---

19  ABC Rural Western Australia, http://www.abc.net.au/news/2014-07-18/the-harrington-family-succession-plan/5606846

Graham had a legal document drawn up so that both he and James had a clear plan for their future. Included in the plan was an out clause for both of them and payout details for James if he left the farm or Graham didn't want him working the farm any more.

James is married to Jacinta, who he met while she was travelling around Australia. Jacinta was a city girl and worked in real estate before she met and married James.

Graham says, "I'm pretty pig-headed and never wanted to share the running of the farm but I was getting older and knew I needed someone to work with me. I wanted to keep farming and do so with someone from my family."

"I chose James because I knew I could work with him. He's my youngest nephew and I like seeing him create success for himself. I let him make a few mistakes but not really big ones. I'll be handing over full control soon but it's hard. Much harder than I thought. I've spent nearly 60 years farming and this is all I know. My body is slowing down but my mind is fine. James knows that and we make it work. He's happy to consult me on decisions and listen to my knowledge and experience. "

"It cost me a lot of money to get the plan in place. I needed help from different professionals over a long period of time to get it right. I'm lucky because my farm has a fairly consistent income. I invested time and money into getting the plan right. It took a lot longer than I thought and we still make changes to it from time to time."

James says that joining Uncle Graham has worked out really well. "I'm glad we got all the hard work done up front, getting the plan in place. I can now farm but still make personal decisions that affect me and my family. There's great freedom in that. I feel like I am in control of my destiny."

"At first, I didn't think it was a big deal having a plan in place but over time, I've seen what can happen if you don't. None of the decisions were made in a single day. These decisions were made over time, 5-6 years, negotiating all the points, but once the agreements were signed, it was such a relief. Of course, you can't get everything exactly how you want it, you have to negotiate."

"My three brothers work with Dad. I am independent of them but some of the best times on the farm have been when we all work together. Just because we farm separately doesn't mean we don't work together. I love farming alongside them. We challenge each other and we have a good time together."

As a former city-dweller, Jacinta didn't have much farming experience prior to marrying James. She says, "I had no idea what I was getting myself into. I was in love with James and wanted to be with him and that meant moving to the farm. We now have three young children and I want to be able to provide for their education and help them get a good start in life."

"I'm not sure our marriage could have survived if James and Graham didn't have a solid plan in place. I've seen other families in the district really struggle with no certainty for their future. Now James and I can make plans as a family for our own future. Yes, we work with Graham, I do the books, which is stressful with young kids underfoot, but I want to feel involved too. I'm really thankful that we have a share of the farm and are involved in the decision making. I feel like we are in control of our future."

## THE LESSONS

The combined lessons that Graham, James and Jacinta share are:

- Get your plan done early
- Have clauses in your plan to deal with changes in circumstances such as one member not wanting to farm any more
- Include everyone in the planning
- It takes much longer than you can imagine to create a good succession plan

- You need to invest time and money into the planning process
- No one will get everything they want, you need to compromise
- You need professional help to sort through the details
- Everyone needs to feel like they have some control over their future

# How Do You Communicate Effectively to Minimise Conflict?

# Chapter 9:

# How Do You Communicate Effectively to Minimise Conflict?

*"Communication is the heartbeat of family business. A business can thrive only in an environment of healthy, open communication and will suffocate and die where communication is blocked, impaired or otherwise constrained."* [20]

You have surely heard of families that started planning for succession and then gave up because of all the disagreements that happened or maybe you know of families that couldn't even start the succession planning process because merely saying the words "succession plan" started fights.

Time and time again, problems with the succession planning process come back to poor communication. While succession planning can bring up issues in a family, good communication can help resolve those issues.

The opportunity to talk opening and communicate effectively by all family members is one of the key factors in whether the succession planning process will be successful or not and how satisfied all parties will be with the outcome.

Communication with professionals assisting in the succession planning process is also critical. When you are working with a range of professional services, you need to have good communication in place between those services and family members.

In creating an environment where open and respectful communication can take place, you should consider the following:

- Hold regular **family meetings**

- Use the succession planning **conversation starters**

- Understand the principles of **effective communication**

---

20  AgWeb - Farm Journal Legacy Project, (2014). *Legacy Workbook.*

- Develop **communication** guidelines
- Identify common **goals** & objectives
- Understand others' **wants**, **needs**, **fears** and **expectations**

These are explored in more detail below and will help you and your family communicate effectively during the succession planning process.

# FAMILY MEETINGS

One of the best ways to start your succession planning process is by having regular family meetings. If you aren't already conducting family meetings as part of your regular business processes, then now is the time to start.

These are integral to clear and open communication and for avoiding misunderstandings. They are an important business process and they become even more critical when you are embarking on the succession planning process.[21]

Here are some tips for organising and managing your family meetings specifically for succession planning.

## Get Agreement

If some family members are reluctant to participate in family meetings, clarify why you are having these meetings and process.

## Organise a Facilitator

An outside facilitator will allow everyone to participate equally and without someone within the family having to take on the role. This creates a more open environment for communication and discussion.

## Include other Professionals as Needed

Depending on where you are at in the succession planning process, you may need to include other professionals in your meetings. The facilitator helps everyone talk openly while your accountant or lawyer etc. provides business expertise.

---

21  AgWeb - Farm Journal Legacy Project, (2014). *Legacy Workbook.*

## Record the Meeting

You need a written record of your meetings. It is best to have an agreement about who will do this before the meeting. Arrange for someone to take detailed notes of the meeting. If you don't have anyone who can take minutes of the meeting, record it on your smart phone and have it transcribed online. It doesn't cost much and it is important to have an accurate record of the decisions made in the meeting.

## Arrange the Meeting Venue

It is important to hold the meeting in a neutral venue. This minimises distractions and maximises the opportunity for family members to contribute. The venue should have a large table to seat everyone.

## Decide Who to Include

All family members should attend the meeting. If family members are not included (such as off-farm children) they feel excluded and it can damage relationships. Off-farm children often contribute useful ideas as they have a different perspective and life experiences. You may also consider including non-family employees.

## Establish Meeting Guidelines

Put some meeting guidelines in place, such as:

- Involve **all** active **family** members
- **Don't personalise** issues (us versus them)
- Stick to the **agenda**, don't rehash old grievances
- **Listen** without judging, hear each other out
- Seek **common ground** and **mutual benefits**

## Outline

Outline specific and attainable objectives for your family meeting.

### Distribute an Agenda

Outline the specific topics to be covered during the meeting and distribute prior to the meeting.

## CONVERSATION STARTERS

If you're having trouble getting the succession planning conversation started, here are some example conversation starters. You can use them to begin the process or utilise them in your succession planning family meeting[22].

- Are you interested in participating in the family operation? (Yes or No)

  If yes, in what capacity?

- Are you prepared to assume that role/responsibility? (Yes or No)

  If no, what will it take to prepare for that role/responsibility?

- Should family members not active in the operation attain/retain an ownership interest in the operation? (Yes or No)

  If no, how should business assets/ownership interests be distributed?

  If you want to be included in the operation, are you willing to personally invest in the business? (Yes or No)

- What is your biggest question or unanswered concern regarding your family's succession intentions?

- Are there other succession-related topics/questions you would like to add to the agenda for your family meeting?

## PRINCIPLES OF EFFECTIVE COMMUNICATION

*" Poor communication is often at the core of abandoned succession  plans or the reason for not starting the process in the first place. "*

Ayesha Hilton

---

22 AgWeb - Farm Journal Legacy Project. *Conversation Starters*.

Communication can be improved if you use the 5 Principles of Good Communication[23]:

## 1. Define Objectives

Clearly define your objectives or the intent of each interaction. Before you engage in a conversation, write an email or make a phone call to clarify the purpose. Conflict often occurs because of misunderstandings and unintended conversational tangents.

## 2. Seek to Understand First

Seek first to understand the other person's point of view. It is easier to grasp an opposing opinion when you start from a point of commonality. When two people stand side by side, they look in the same direction; from there, it is easier to explore what's different about their perspectives.

## 3. Be Open to New Ideas

There are many roads that lead to the same destination, so be open to alternative routes. Discussions are more productive—and fun—when we remember that there is no single right way to do anything.

## 4. Different Perspectives Can Yield Greater Results

Acknowledge that it takes complementary qualities to create a successful operation which can stand the test of time. Misunderstandings may be based on motivation, abilities, skills or vision, all of which may serve as the balancing characteristics necessary to build a business bigger than self.

## 5. It's Okay to Disagree

Please know that there is nothing wrong with disagreeing with each other. How's this for an interesting idea? If two people agree on everything, one of them is unnecessary! There is great value in discussion about differing perspectives and ideas – as long as no punches are thrown.

Use these five principles to create a consistent communication strategy. It is important to have regular family meetings and that they are scheduled at a time convenient for most participants.

---

23  AgWeb - Farm Journal Legacy Project, (2014). *Legacy Workbook.*

## COMMUNICATION GUIDELINES

Establish guidelines that will help keep the lines of communication open and respectful. In your succession plan, you should also have a documented communications plan that describes how your family is going to communicate about succession planning and transition as well as how you will manage and resolve disputes.

## IDENTIFY COMMON GOALS

*" Succession planning means turning intentions into goals, goals into actions and actions into results. "* [24]

Communication and understanding can be enhanced by identifying and agreeing on common goals for the succession planning process.[25] Here are the most common goals:

- Keeping farm business **ownership** in the family

- Maintaining the business' **profitability**

- Providing **liquidity** for the owner or estate

- Providing **financial security** for the family

- Minimising the owner's current **tax liability**

- Maintaining family **harmony**

There may be limits on your ability to achieve these goals if they conflict with each other. For example, depending on your situation, keeping ownership in the family may not be feasible if no one in the family wants to manage the farm but the goals serve a purpose when communicating about succession planning.

---

24  AgWeb - Farm Journal Legacy Project, (2014). *Legacy Workbook.*

25  AgWeb - Farm Journal Legacy Project, (2014). *Legacy Workbook.*

## TRY TO UNDERSTAND EACH OTHER

Effective communication in your family will help you understand the wants, needs, fears and expectations of other family members. This in turn will help you develop a succession plan that takes these into consideration while minimising conflict. (For more information on understanding each other's needs, see *Chapter 10: How Do You Understand Everyone's Needs?*)

*As you know, communication is vital to a successful succession process. Next we will share a case study where the older family members really want their children to have off-farm careers and what happens when one of those children insists on returning to farming. After the case study, we will look at how to understand everyone's needs in the family by looking at generational differences.*

# Case Study 9:

# Parents Encourage Children to have Off-Farm Careers

*" My parents didn't really want me to follow in their footsteps, they wanted me to have a career off the farm. I tried to do want they wanted but the farm was always calling to me. They were happy for me to take over the farming operations but they were worried that if they gave me the land, I might sell it and keep the profits and disadvantage my sisters. "*

Sometimes, parents encourage their children to seek careers outside of farming. These parents know only too well that precarious nature of farming and they want their children to have more security and less stress. Some children take their parents advice and build a good career for themselves off the farm. Others have farming in their blood and can't stay away.

### Charlie's Story

My parents always encouraged my sisters and me to have a life off the farm. They wanted us to go to university or, in my case, to get a trade. They wanted us to see what life was like away from the farm. They didn't want us to go through what they had to on the farm – the droughts, floods, fires, stress and lack of security.

So after high school, I got an apprenticeship as an electrician. I didn't mind the work and I was good at it but I always found myself longing for the farm and the freedom of working on the land for myself. I asked my parents if I could come home and work with them.

My parents could see that I wanted to make farming my career so Mum and Dad said I could take over the farm but they were worried about me selling the farm later on and keeping all the money, thereby disadvantaging my sisters.

I got some professional advice about the best way to deal with this. One solution was separating the land ownership from the operation of the business. I could take over the operation of the business while my parents still owned the land. This didn't even occur to me until I got advice. I'd always thought that I would have to own the land if I wanted to run the farm.

So we separated the farming operations from the land ownership. This gave us greater flexibility. Originally, my parents owned the land in partnership and I leased the land and ran the farming business.

We later established a unit trust to own the land and we set up a company as a trustee with the three of us as directors of the company. Not only has this been a safe way to manage the ownership of the land (my parents don't have to worry about me selling the land and running off with the cash) but it has also given me invaluable experience in how a company operates.

Now I lease the farm from the trust and my parents get a regular income, security and reassurance. Over time, the plan is for me to buy out their units in the trust and for my parents to leave cash for my sisters in their will. I feel like this is the best possible solution and outcome for me and my family.

## THE LESSONS

- Often succession planning is delayed because the business and ownership are tied up in the same structure - parents often believe that handing over the business also means handing over land ownership

- You can separate ownership of land from the operation of the business

- Parents can feel more secure in handing over just the business side of things while retaining land ownership

# How Do You Understand Everyone's Needs?

# Chapter 10:

# How Do You Understand Everyone's Needs?

*" So much suffering and resentment arises from
simple misunderstandings and wrong assumptions.
We need to be clear about everyone's needs and expectations
to avoid family conflict. "*

Ayesha Hilton

If anything is going to tear a family apart, create rifts and damage relationships its succession planning and wills. In order to stop this happening, the solution is to create a sound succession plan in advance of trouble.

If everyone has a good understanding of what's going to happen, when it will happen and why things are being done a certain way, you will have a much more peaceful family and business life.

Much of the drama surrounding succession planning comes from misunderstandings and unmet expectations. Understanding other people's needs and expectations is very important in succession planning and why we have devoted a whole chapter to this topic.

In family farms there are generally three types of stakeholders in at least two generations:

- **Parents** (Main Asset Owners)

- **On-Farm** Children and their families

- **Off-Farm** Children and their families

Each of these stakeholders has different needs and expectations and these may be in conflict with each other. So, regardless of which one of these stakeholders you are, it's important to understand the viewpoints, aspirations and concerns of the other parties involved.

If all family members have a mutual understanding of these differences, there is more chance of developing a succession plan that everyone can live happily with – though you have to realise that a good succession plan is when everyone is a little unhappy, you don't want one party happy and the rest very unhappy.

# HOW DO THE GENERATIONS DIFFER?

*" When the older generation are hell bent on a top down approach and the younger generation are desperate for a bottom up approach the issue provides the opportunity for family conflict before succession planning even begins." [26]*

You may have noticed that each generation has a different perspective on how things are in the world. They have a different work ethic, a preferred way of doing things and different priorities. Understanding these differences will make it easier for you during the succession planning process. We recommend that each generation try and understand the other generations involved.

We are all products of time and upbringing. You don't need to agree with each other's values and expectations but you do need to understand them.

## Traditionalists (born 1918-1945)

**Famous Traditionalists:**

- Joan Sutherland

- Robert (Bob) Hawke

- Paul Hogan

- David Malouf

- John Howard

- Barry Humphries

- Paul Keating

- Arthur Boyd

- Elizabeth Tailor

---

26  University of Ottawa – Faculty of Medicine (2014). *Generational differences.*

**Key Influences:**

*   World War II
*   Korean War
*   Great Depression
*   Space Age

Growing up in the great depression and in war fostered a sense of fatalism and powerlessness. People expected little and held onto any job they could find. Forces beyond their control affected their destiny and then the Second World War came. Friends died in large numbers. Men were away at war so delayed marriage until after the conflict, leading to the baby boom. [27]

**Preferred Work Environment:**

*   Conservative
*   Hierarchical
*   Clear chain of command
*   Top-down management

**Key to Working with Traditionalists:**

*   Work is not supposed to be enjoyable or fun
*   Like to follow rules and understand procedures
*   Frustrated by perceived lack of discipline, respect, logic and structure
*   Tend to be conservative in workplace

## Baby Boomers (born 1946 –1964)

**Famous Baby Boomers:**

*   Peter Carey
*   James Blundell
*   Tommy Emmanuel

---

27  University of Ottawa – Faculty of Medicine (2014). *Generational differences.*

- Kay Cottee
- Judy Davis
- Geoffrey Rush
- Allan Border
- Bill Clinton
- Meryl Streep

**Key Influences:**

- Civil Rights
- Vietnam War
- Sexual Revolution
- Cold War/Russia
- Space Travel

The parents of baby boomers had worked in the war effort and were independent, strong willed and used to hardship. After the war ended, couples made up for the delay in child-bearing and why so many children were born in this period.

Baby boomers grew up in an era of optimism. They were also the first generation to grow up with television and they had more access to education than their own parents had had. These days, many baby boomers are caring for aging parents and are often sandwiched between obligations to their parents and their children.

**Preferred Work Environment:**

- Conservative
- "Flat" organisational hierarchy
- Democratic
- Humane
- Equal opportunity
- Warm, friendly environment

**Key to Working with Baby Boomers:**

- They want their ideas and their life to matter
- Expect to be valued in the workplace
- Defined by their career
- Respond well to recognition and attention
- Don't take criticism well
- Need flexibility, attention and freedom

## Generation X (born 1965 – 1974)

**Famous Gen X-ers:**

- Eric Bana
- Toni Collette
- Rachel Griffiths
- Cate Blanchett
- Hugh Jackman
- Shane Warne
- Barak Obama
- Jennifer Lopez

**Key Influences:**

- Single Parent Families
- Y2K
- Energy Crisis
- Downsizing
- End of the Cold War
- Working mothers
- Increased divorce rates

Generation X were born in a time of financial insecurity with high interest rates and high unemployment. They were the first generation to develop strong computer skills. Due to the fragile job market, they were often worried about job security and would work long hours to get a raise, promotion, career development and respect. Many delayed having children until later in life and had fewer children.

**Preferred Work Environment:**

- Conservative
- Functional, positive, fun
- Efficient
- Fast paced and flexible
- Informal
- Access to leadership
- Access to information

**Key to Working with Generation X:**

- Want independence in the workplace and informality
- Need time to pursue non-work passions
- Like to have fun at work
- Enjoy using the latest technology

## Gen Y 1978 – 1994 (born c. 1974 – 1997, 23 year span)

**Famous Gen Y-ers:**

- Delta Goodrem
- Ian Thorpe
- Lleyton Hewitt
- Ashton Kutcher
- Serena Williams

**Key Influences:**

- Digital media
- Child focused world
- Terrorist attacks
- 9/11

The Gen Y generation loves digital communication. They resent being talked down to (who doesn't?). They love to give and receive feedback. They have a good sense of fun and appreciate humour. They love interesting and interactive learning environments. They have a great team spirit and enjoy socialising with colleagues. Many grew up in divorced families. Interestingly, they are the first generation of kids to have schedules – they do lots of extra-curricular activities.

**Preferred Work Environment:**

- Collaborative
- Achievement-oriented
- Highly creative
- Positive
- Diverse
- Fun, flexible, want continuous feedback

**Key to Working with Generation Y:**

- Like a team oriented workplace
- Want to work with bright, creative people
- Expect to be treated respectfully
- Need rationale for work
- Need variety
- Like to be acknowledge for excellence
- Take technology for granted

## Generation Z (born 1998 – present)

There isn't as much information about Gen Z as they are still relatively young but given the digital era they are growing up in, the internet is not technology, it's a normal part of life. They are very similar to the Gen Ys thus far but they're only young, so who knows what they will be like as adults and parents. But time will tell.

## HEARING THE DIFFERENT VOICES

As you can see above, there are a lot of differences between the generations. Even just having an idea of the different events and circumstances that have influenced their thinking, whether it be the Great Depression or 9/11, gives you a better understanding of each generation.

This can help make it much easier to understand and even accept the needs, opinions and expectations of the other people in your family when it comes to succession planning.

Here are some of the common things we have heard from different family members about succession planning. These might give you an insight into how someone in your family might be feeling and thinking.

### Parents

Parents may wish to pass the farm on to the next generation and begin the process of planning for their own retirement.

Here are some of the comments from parents:

- *"I know it is time to pass on the farm but I don't want family conflict."*

- *"We need money to secure our retirement but don't want to burden our children with too much debt."*

- *"We've spent our lifetime growing the farm but now we don't know if we will have enough money to retire on."*

- *"I hate to even bring this up but what will happen to the farm if one of the kids gets divorced?"*

- *"I understand that the kids can purchase the farm over time from the business profits but if something happens to prevent those payments, our retirement income will be seriously affected."*

- *"I am not sure that the kids have the skills and knowledge to take over the business at this point."*

- *"I am pleased to pass on a legacy that has taken generations to build but I don't want the kids putting the property on the market as soon as it is transferred."*

- *"I think they want us off the farm and we aren't ready to go."*

- *"We've got three boys that are all very keen on farming and we've got one farm."*

- *"Now all of a sudden you have three decision-makers and each one is pulling in his direction."*

- *"We just kept putting succession planning in the too-hard basket but at the same time, I knew we had to try and do something."*

- *"Families are wonderfully loyal until they're not and then the shit hits the fan."*

- *"Retirement for me is being able to continue doing exactly what I am doing now and, most importantly, enjoying it."*

- *"When it comes to succession planning, it's often the bond between the mother and daughter-in-law that faces the toughest test."*

- *"When you're the mother-in-law and you get this new young girl coming into the family, it feels like she's taking over."*

- *"We want to see younger farmers on the land because the alternative is just more factory farms."*

- *"I'm just thinking of scaling back, not ever really stopping what I'm doing."*

- *"We want our children to understand that they are in business. If they love farming, it's got to be a separate mentality to the ownership of the land. I want them to come to realise that value is there because of the things we're doing - so there is a reason for them to want to learn."*

## On-Farm Children

On-farm children may want to take over the day to day running of the farm or at least be given more decision making power and financial security.

Here are some of the comments from on-farm children:

- *"I have all these great ideas but I never get to do any of them."*

- *"Dad won't let me do anything I want to do, I am just a hired hand."*

- *"We would love to take over the farm from Mum and Dad but we don't want to be burdened by too much debt."*

- *"We've worked for years for a lower wage than our brothers/sisters have been able to earn off the farm. How will this be recognised?"*

- *"We need to know what Mum and Dad's intentions are. There must be some certainty about the future. We need to think about our financial security for the sake of our own children."*

- *"I know Mum and Dad need some retirement money but I can't write them out a big cheque and take over the debts."*

- *"I want to professionalise the business but Dad says preparing a strategic plan is a waste of time."*

- *"Taking the land away from the business is going to make me look at a completely new ball game now because I sort of had the view that the land was my business. That's my income. But I'm now looking at it in a different way and because of that, it opens up a whole chapter."*

## Off-Farm Children

Off-farm children may be worried that because they don't live and work on the farm, they might miss out on some of their "rightful" inheritance.

Here are some of the comments from off-farm children:

- *"It's not fair that my brother inherits the whole farm. While I might not live on the farm, I should be entitled to inherit some of Mum and Dad's assets."*

- *"I've never felt the farm owed me anything because I once lived there."*

- *"This fair versus equal issue is not always easy."*

- *"Traditionally, women have been asked to make room for the men of the family."*

## Ask!

The best way to find out what everyone is thinking and feeling is to ask them. You don't need to be a mind reader and you need to be very wary of making assumptions. If everyone can share what they really think, feel and want, succession planning becomes a whole lot easier.

*It's interesting to see how all the generations differ. Adopt a curious attitude rather than being judgemental (we know, it's easier said than done). Next we will share a case study about a daughter-in-law and her struggles. After the case study, look at ways to deal with fairness and equity issues that come up especially between on-farm and off-farm siblings.*

# Case Study 10:

# The Daughter-in-Law Syndrome

*" We invested time and money into succession planning but my parents-in-law didn't really want to go through with the transition of assets and control.*
*Now it's the end of an era for farming in my family and that breaks my heart."*

When a son marries and the new daughter-in-law joins the family business, this can change the family dynamics. Known as the daughter–in-law (DIL) syndrome, this change in family dynamics often means that the daughter–in-law gets the blame for any disharmony or for a change in priorities with regards to how funds are budgeted and spent.

Many daughters–in-law are tertiary educated and can bring many skills to the business. This may be daunting and intimidating to the older generation who may not be as well educated. The DIL may even have a really good understanding of things like derivative swaps, grain markets and technology skills.

In farming, you live above the shop, so to speak. It's not common outside of farming where the father and son work ten hours a day together, six days a week. Their social scene is overlapping at the football, netball and social BBQ. This might be fine when you are a single man living at home with your parents but for the new wife, this may bring a whole lot of unexpected challenges.

Bringing new energy and skills into the business is actually a positive thing. It doesn't have to be a negative thing to have a DIL. We have devoted more space to this case study as it is such a common story.

## Margaret's Story

I was born in a town in western Victoria and grew up on my parents' farm nearby. I loved farm life as a child and enjoyed having animals to look after and helping Mum and Dad.

When I finished school and went to find work I always felt better when I was working in a rural area rather than the city. I took a job about 30 minutes from my parents' farm about a year after leaving school. It was at a rural merchandiser doing secretarial work and some merchandising. I really enjoyed the interaction with the rural customers and it felt right to be with my community.

While I was enjoying a holiday with friends in Perth, I met a nice man called James who was from the Geraldton area in Western Australia. He, like myself, was from a family farm. We had a lot to talk about and spent a lot of time discussing farming and the opportunities and barriers that living away from city life presents.

We communicated for around six months before I made the trip to Geraldton. It was a bit of a culture shock. When he said he lived just out of Geraldton, I didn't think that meant 120kms away! My visions of a quiet lunch together by the water in Geraldton a couple of times a week soon vanished.

As James worked with his parents on the farm and as I was from a similar but smaller all cropping farm back east, I was a bit shocked at how the distribution of labour was working. It seemed like James had quite a large debt from a farm purchase not long before and the parents had all the control over the farming decisions. James also has an older and younger sister who have finished school and moved away.

As our relationship reached the one year anniversary, we started to talk about where we were heading as a couple and when I could move to Western Australia. At times I didn't feel too welcome by James's parents but when I mentioned that to James he said that every prospective daughter-in-law feels that way. We also discussed a family succession plan and James suggested that the farm advisor had started the process.

I moved west in the March before planting started. The planting went well and the crop was sown on time with ample moisture. I was busy helping James move machinery and running the house. The little workers cottage that we set up in was five kilometres from James's parent's place, so I didn't see them too much.

My parents came over in late July that year to help plant some trees and shrubs around the sandy area I had as a garden. James surprised my parents and myself when he proposed at a family dinner in Geraldton.

Even though we had discussed getting married before I moved west, it was still a bit of a shock. I was happy that he felt we belonged together and that we brought out the best in each other. We planned to get married back in western Victoria at the start of the following January. I was busy getting things sorted remotely from the west, while my mum and dad organised the crew in the east.

Harvest comes earlier in the west than back at home. We started harvest on the 10th of October that year and we were completed by the 20th of November. This gave us four weeks to get everything sorted out before we flew back to Victoria just before Christmas and then we had three weeks after Christmas before the wedding. The wedding went well and James's parents seemed to have a good time while over in Victoria.

When we got back to Western Australia after our honeymoon there seemed to be more stress in the family unit. There had been rain while we were away and the summer weeds were out of control. James could only spray at night due to the temperature in summertime. I felt like James and I were being blamed for the weeds being out of control as we had been away from the farm for so long. It reinforced what James and I had been speaking about before we got married; we needed a strategic document to define roles and also to have a process of family meetings.

The main sheds where the machinery was kept was located at the in-laws' farm. James would be there and have a morning or afternoon cuppa with his parents (normal in farming families) and this was when most of the management decisions were discussed or decided.

The season produced below average yields and I still felt some blame as the summer weeds caused problems at planting and therefore crop establishment was poor. I kept asking James about the strategic document and he said we would all discuss it at the advisors post-harvest meeting.

All the family members were present at the advisors meeting in Geraldton in mid-January. The financial figures were below average and there was quite a heated discussion about why and the direction of the business. The strategic document wasn't on the agenda and I felt that since it was my first advisors meeting, I should sit and learn the dynamics of the family.

In June that year, James and I announced that we were having a baby in December. We had a healthy baby girl on Boxing Day. Time seemed to slip away and before I knew it my baby was three and I was pregnant again with twins this time. I was hesitantly excited but it meant I needed to go to Perth to have the babies.

We had a little girl and boy in the July. Having the twins seemed to cause more stress on the family unit. James had to juggle looking after our older daughter while spraying and getting ready for harvest. We needed a bigger car to fit all the car seats and luggage that comes with twins. I felt so bad because we basically had to go begging to James's parents for a new car. I wanted a four-wheel drive so I could catch up with James while he was working so that he could see the kids. This caused huge stress as James and I had to borrow money separately from the farm to buy the car.

After that event, I suggested we needed professional help with the strategic document and the farm succession plan, as the advisor had basically put it in the too hard basket. We did some preliminary work online and also sent paperwork back to Melbourne for the succession planner before our face to face meeting.

We met the succession planner in Geraldton and all my fears started coming true. James's mother was very upset that we needed a succession plan and said that it was their farm and they would do with it what they wanted. I immediately froze. I remembered all the bad succession plans we used to talk about when I was living with my parents. Now, here I was, in the middle of a succession planning disaster myself.

That was two years ago now. The cost of that meeting was not only the financial cost of $4,500 to engage the succession planner but more importantly, it was the damage to the family unit.

I no longer go to the annual advisors meetings and successive poor seasons have taken a toll on the viability of the farm. After the last advisors meeting it was decided to sell the farm as James was unable to purchase the farm from his parents due to lack of equity.

James and I have discussed our future. We have three loving healthy children that love the rural aspect of life. James has always worked on the farm and has a management degree that is 20 years old. He has been looking at manager's positions that will be better paid than we are now and also gives us a holiday.

I will be sad when we leave our little farmhouse. I put so many hours into the garden and surrounding areas. I feel sad that my children will most likely not be able to be farmers even if they wanted to. It is the end of the road for five generations of farming from my side of the family.

I hope my story can help others overcome their own farm succession issues through reading about my personal experiences before it is too late. Please be up front and keep the conversation going even though it is hard and sometimes unrewarding. Think about your children and how you want them to enjoy where they live.

## The Lessons

- A poor or non-existent succession plan can spell disaster and the end of an era after generations of farmers

- Not having a plan in place can cause a lot of stress for everyone involved and can lead to strained relationships

- Succession planning is a process that takes time and commitment

# How Do You Deal with Fairness & Equity Issues?

# Chapter 11:

# How Do You Deal with Fairness & Equity Issues?

*"In succession planning, the aim is to treat family members fairly but not necessarily equally. It also involves compromise on everyone's part. A good succession plan is where everyone is a little dissatisfied – that means there has been compromise and no single person has everything they want."*

### Nick Shady

You can't have a succession planning book without addressing fairness and equity. Time and time again, succession planning falls over when issues of fairness and equity aren't addressed.

Concerns arise about how to address the difference between siblings that work on the farm and those who don't. The fact is that some siblings contribute to the success of the farm and some don't.

Farming families have to deal with the practical realities of fairness and equity when dividing up the land when it means that no one has an economically viable farm. Family conflict often arises when people do not feel that they are being treated equally and fairly.

Mum and Dad may disagree about what is fair. Off-farm siblings may feel that they are due a fair and equal share of the farm and its profits. On-farm siblings may feel ripped off when they've worked so hard on the farm for so long and their off-farm brothers or sisters want an equal share of the farm.

It can seem like an impossible task to treat all family members fairly and equitably. How do you put a value on the work that an adult child has put into helping run the family farm with the sibling who has left the farm to have their own career?

Different families will have varying perspectives on the issue of fairness and equity but regardless of your views, it is something that will need to be discussed openly and respectfully. Everyone wants to be treated fairly and by discussing these issues, you can hopefully avoid a lot of misunderstandings and resentment.

Here are some questions you can think about and discuss with your family:

- **Do we need to treat all siblings equally?**

  If one or two children have put their whole life into the farm, while the others have had their education paid for by the farm and have their own lives and career off the farm, why should the farm be split up to pay them out. Many farming families have gotten into serious trouble and debt trying to treat all siblings equally. Does everyone deserve an equal inheritance in the farm and is it fair and reasonable to split the farm up?

- **Do we need to pay off-farm family members at the start?**

  Do we need to commit to paying off-farm family members at the start of a partnership so that those on the farm do not have to pay for the capital improvement later on? This would mean that all parties benefit from the parents' assets at the same time and are equally responsible for the welfare of their parents at retirement. This provides a practical way of treating children equally at the start of the succession planning process with the proviso that all children are responsible for contributing to their parents' retirement.

- **Is educating off-farm children as valuable as receiving land?**

  Paying for a child's university education so that they can have a successful career off the farm is incredibly valuable and many consider it as valuable as inheriting land because you can never lose your education but you can lose your farm. Educating on farm children is also important as education can help them run a successful farm enterprise.

- **Too many children, not enough land, so who should inherit?**

  Often, the oldest boy will inherit the farm because it isn't viable to split it up among all the siblings. The logic is that the girls will marry farmers and they'll be okay and the youngest boy might not be into farming. However, there is a case for keeping an open mind about who should inherit and how it should be structured. Some families can afford to purchase farms for each of the children but what if this isn't an option and dividing up the farm means that no part is economically viable?

- **Do parents have an obligation to leave an inheritance for their children?**

  Parents actually don't have any obligation to provide an inheritance for their children but they usually want to leave something for them. Is providing an opportunity for education and a successful life off the farm worth as much as land inheritance?

- **Where does earning capacity and asset value come into it?**

  The earning capacity of a farm and its resale value varies according to the current season, commodity markets and the property market. There may be times when the farm is earning a lot of money but the value of the land asset is low or vice versa.

## POSSIBLE SOLUTIONS FOR DEALING WITH EQUITY AND FAIRNESS

There are a number of ways your family can address the issue of fairness and equity:[28]

- **Buy/Sell Agreements**

  Parents can outline specific sale terms, ownership restrictions, triggering events and timelines regarding the farm's various assets. On-farm siblings have some assurance they will inherit the farm, while off-farm siblings know they will receive a previously agreed upon amount of money.

- **Individual Insurance Policies**

  Parents can take out individual insurance policies so that upon their death, the off-farm siblings inherit this cash, while on-farm siblings receive the farm assets.

---

28  PNC Bank (2011). *Succession Planning on the Farm.*

- **Wills & Trusts**

  Parents can structure the distribution of their assets to take into account previously distributed assets and the transfer of assets to off-farm children. For example, if the parents have a share portfolio, they could leave that to the off-farm children.

- **Financial Assistance for Off-Farm Heirs**

  Parents could provide financial assistance for off-farm siblings in various ways, including:
  - Pay for their education which will increase the child's capacity to earn an income.
  - Providing financial assistance in setting up a business not connected to farm assets.
  - Contribute to a deposit for a house.
  - Assist with the purchase of off-farm investments such as shares or property.

## REMEMBERING THE VIABILITY OF THE FARM OPERATION

All decisions of fairness and equity should be made with the farm's viability in mind. The financial security and the economic viability of the farm are critical. Carving up the farm so that everyone feels fairly treated is not a good solution if it means that no one can actually have a sustainable business.

*Now you've got a better idea about the difference between fairness and equity. Next we will share a case study where a husband dies and leaves the wife penniless with a newborn baby (this is a pretty sad story). After the case study, we will talk about the most boring topic in this book – business structures – but hang in here with us, we've made it simple to understand and easy to read.*

# Case Study 11:

# Husband Dies & Wife Left Penniless

*" I didn't realise that I would end up a single parent and a widow with no assets and no support. Life hasn't worked out like I imagined and I'm bitter and angry about how my son and I have been treated by my husband's parents. "*

You never know when you or your spouse will die. Perhaps it will be in old age, with all your ducks lined up nicely but it could just as easily be sudden. If you are not prepared for the eventuality of death, you risk leaving your family in hardship.

## Cathy's Story

Will and I had only been married two years when he got bowel cancer. We were pregnant with our first child at the time. Will became ill very quickly and died within four months – only two weeks after our son, Joshua, was born.

So, there I was with a two week old baby burying my husband. I was a widow and a single parent. I was devastated. My dream of a family life was shattered. My family were all interstate and I felt all alone in the middle of nowhere.

I was living on the farm with Will's parents at the time. Will and I had our own house on one of the farming properties. Will's parents were grieving, I know, but they made me feel really unwelcome. It was like seeing my son, who was a mini version of Will, just broke their heart.

They never spent any time with us. I had no income and had to go on a government pension. I felt so uncomfortable that I ended up moving to the local town where I rented a small house for Joshua and me.

We've survived but things have been tight. I don't have an education and I live in a small community with few jobs. I work in the local take away place and smell of rancid oil most of the time.

When Will died, his parents assured me that they would pay for Joshua's education and that he would be taken care of. Josh is about to start high school and the promise of assistance has never eventuated.

I would like Joshua to have a good education but that would mean going to school in a larger town. There aren't many opportunities where we live but I can't afford to rent somewhere more expensive or pay school fees.

I loved Will and still miss him but I'm also angry because by dying he ruined my life as well. I've struggled as a single parent to provide for our son. I've had no support from Will's parents and I don't know what's in store for Josh. I never expected that I'd be almost destitute, broke and have no financial security if Will died. We never talked about it. He would be horrified that Josh and I had been left to survive in this way.

## THE LESSONS

- Once again, the lesson here is that life can change at any moment and any of us can be killed or injured

- If you are not prepared, you are risking leaving your family in real hardship

- Go and get life insurance for you and your spouse – that way, if one of you dies, the other has some money to survive on

# How Do You Choose the Best Business Structure?

# Chapter 12:

# How Do You Choose the Best Business Structure?

*" Equity ownership among a family needs to be structured to ensure the business can be effectively managed on a day-to-day basis. These issues should be dealt with early in the business transition process. If left unresolved they can cause problems for future owners, especially where the property and business values increase as a result of their decisions and efforts. "* [29]

In developing your succession plan, you will need to think about how to structure the farming operation. How you structure the business will have a big impact on the control and transfer of assets, as well as the taxation and stamp duty payable.

*Disclaimer: The caveat for this chapter is seek professional help. The information contained here is only a guide so that you have an overview of the different options available.*

In transferring control and ownership of assets in your succession plan, there are a number of different business arrangements you can use. There are four main ways you can structure your farm business. Each of these structures has their advantages and disadvantages.

The four main structures are:

- Sole Trader

- Partnership

- Trust

- Company

---

29  PNC Bank (2011). *Succession Planning on the Farm.*

In addition to this, you may like to create a self-managed super fund (SMSF) that may own some of your assets.

There is no single structure that is always the best solution. The most appropriate solution for your family will depend on your personal circumstances. Often, families choose a combination of at least two of these structures.

There are a number of factors that will determine which arrangements are most suitable for your family, including:

- Level of **control** each party wants to have over the farm in terms of management decisions and purchase and sale of assets

- Impact on the **management structure,** dealing with **conflicts of interest** and the **decision-making process**

- **Taxation and stamp duty implications** of the various structures

- **Costs associated** with the various business structures

- **Protection** of personal assets from **liabilities** of the farm business

- Ease and flexibility of **changing ownership**

- Ability to **raise funds** for the farming business

- Ability of the structure to deal with the effects of **death, divorce and relationship breakdown**

- Suitability of different structures for **asset ownership** and **business operation**

- Managing **non-farm income** as part of the succession plan

- Capacity of **new members** to buy into the business

All of these need to be considered in conjunction with your overall succession planning goals and with sound advice from your team of professionals that understand the taxation and succession planning impacts of the different structures.[30]

---

30  Information on this section has been taken from various sources, including Weir, G. (2014). *Production Horticulture Farm Succession Planning Toolbox.*

Now this is a dry subject for many of us to read or talk about but it's really important to understand the different potential business structures you could use in your succession planning. We've tried to make the topic, if not interesting, at least easy to understand.

# SOLE TRADER

This is the most simple of business structures where a single person controls the business. One person is responsible for all business decisions and financial matters.

## Advantages

- One person controls all decisions
- Easy to setup up and operate
- Low cost to set up and administer
- Simple business structure
- Taxation advantages when profits are low

## Disadvantages

- One personal is legally responsible for all aspects of the business
- Does not allow for multiple people to be involved in the decision making
- Does not lend itself to succession planning because of only one person being in control
- Debts and losses cannot be shared
- Raising finance is dependent on personal wealth
- Private assets such as home, land, contents and vehicles, are at risk if the business goes into debt
- Taxation disadvantages when profits are higher
- Selling ownership of the business may be difficult

# PARTNERSHIP

This is the most common business structure used by farmers. A partnership is an agreement between family members to share in the profit of the business. It is relatively simple to set up and administer and because of this is less expensive to operate than say a company or trust. The partnership relies heavily on all partners being able to work together cooperatively and with trust.[31]

## Advantages

- Provides the opportunity for shared management

- Is affordable to implement and administer (depending on stamp duty issues)

- Provides joint ownership of assets

- Existing assets can easily be transferred to family members entering the partnership

- All partners contribute to the capacity to raise finance

- Losses and legal responsibilities are shared among the partners

- Tax advantages may exist if partners are from the same family

## Disadvantages

- All partners are responsible for the debts of the partnership, even if they are incurred by another partner

- You can lose your private assets as your home, land, contents and vehicles to settle debts of the partnership (personal assets need to be protected from potential liability)

- May not provide a clear distinction between personal and business activities

- Assets contributed to the partnership may cause capital gains tax problems

- A partnership does not own assets directly – each member of the partnership shares the ownership

- If a partner decides to dissolve the business, it may effectively end the business

---

31  Weir, G. (2014). *Production Horticulture Farm Succession Planning Toolbox.*

- As the business develops, personalities may clash and there may be disputes over operations and profit sharing

- Partnership assets can cause problems on the death of a partner and there is the possibility of challenges to the will

- If land is included in the partnership assets and is owned as joint tenants, then the land will automatically pass to the remaining joint tenants on death, regardless of your will

- Problems can occur in the event of death, disablement or divorce of one of the partners

- Partnerships end whenever the membership changes, which makes it relatively inflexible for changing membership

## TRUST

Farming families often utilise trusts in their business structures because they provide important asset protection against liabilities. Basically, a trust is a relationship (usually expressed in the form of a deed) where the trustee (a person or another entity) controls a business and/or assets to the benefit of the beneficiaries (the people or entities receiving the profits).

"The trustee is the legal owner of the trust's assets but these assets can only be dealt with according to the powers given in the trust deed."[32]

Most family farming enterprises use the trust structure operate it as a discretionary trust. This means that the trustee has total power to determine how the income and/or assets of the trust are to be distributed to the beneficiaries. Decisions are based on their discretion, so to speak.

The other most common form of the trust structure is the unit trust where unit holders (for example individuals or several discretionary family trusts) hold units in the trust (similar to shares in a company), which entitles each unit holder a determined share of income and/or capital.

You will definitely need legal advice if you want to establish a trust. You need to consider choosing the trustee carefully as they have the power to control all the assets of the trust as well as the ability to appoint and remove other trustees. In

---

32  Weir, G. (2014). *Production Horticulture Farm Succession Planning Toolbox.*

most cases, the original appointers are parties whose family will benefit from the trust. Generally, having a number of joint appointers, possibly including an independent appointer, provides greater asset protection and succession planning benefits, so it is preferable to avoid having a sole appointer.[33]

Alternatively, a company could be made the appointer. This protects the assets of the trustee and provides a structure whereby the family can manage the business and a company is normally formed to act as trustee. This means that family members can control the company (and therefore the decisions of the trustee) by holding shares in the company and as shareholders, appointing family members as company directors, who in turn make the decisions effectively as the trustee of the trust.[34]

## Advantages

- The trustee retains control of management and assets and separates management from ownership

- Protection of beneficiaries' assets from the liabilities of the trust (business)

- The trustee has flexibility regarding the distribution of income and capital

- Flexibility of entry and exit with a unit trust

- Trust assets are outside the wills of family members unless the trust is a unit trust (this reduces the risk of challenges to a will)

- The trust deed can be tailored to the needs of principals and beneficiaries

- The trust has perpetual existence and does not cease with the death of a beneficiary

- Some tax minimisation and flexibility

- Ease of succession

- Less regulation than a company and easier to wind up

- Privacy of business information

---

33  Weir, G. (2014). Production Horticulture Farm Succession Planning Toolbox. GRDC, Judy Wilkinson & Lyn Sykes (2007). A Guide to Succession Planning: Sustaining Families and Farms. Fleming Muntz Solicitors - Albury-Wodonga Legal Firm, (2008). Succession and Estate Planning for Country Clients.

34  Weir, G. (2014). *Production Horticulture Farm Succession Planning Toolbox.*

## Disadvantages

- Sole manager of trust property by the trustee if a company is used as trustee

- Higher establishment costs than for partnerships

- Capital gains tax may be due if land is transferred to the trust

- Beneficiaries are not legal owners of trust property and therefore cannot will these assets

- Profits distributed to children may be taxed at higher rates

- Trusts may include beneficiaries that are no longer appropriate for the existing business circumstances

- Can be very difficult to dismantle

# PROPRIETARY LIMITED COMPANY

A proprietary limited company is commonly known as a private company and is created through legislation. A company is a separate legal entity and makes all of its decisions and enters into all contracts associated with operating the farm business through its directors. The company may also own the assets of the business although this is not always necessary as they could be leased from another entity.

If you set up a company for your business, you become a shareholder in the company and profits are paid as dividends. Shareholders have the power to elect directors and share in the capital of the company if it is liquidated. However, shareholders do not have the right to participate in day to day decision making or the assets while the company is still operating.

Due to the complexity and expense of establishing and administering a company, most small family farming operations do not use the company structure unless they are using the company as the trustee of a family trust as described above.

## Advantages

- Limited liability of shareholders can protect the private assets of family members and is limited to the money invested in the business (unless you personally guarantee debts)

- Ownership of assets can be transferred through the sale of shares without affecting the operation of the business

- The business survives the death of family members

- Shared management where two or more directors are involved

- More suitable for larger farming operations where non-family members are involved in the ownership of the business

- Capital gains tax on the transfer of assets to the company can be deferred

- Greater access to capital as lenders look favourably on the limited liability

- A company can own property

## Disadvantages

- Cost of setting up the company will be higher than a partnership

- Lack of privacy of financial information

- Directors may be held liable for company debts in some circumstances

- The transfer or sale of shares can be difficult in a private company

- There are limitations on distributing income

- Ownership of allotments of land held by the company cannot be transferred to individual members, only shares in the company can be transferred

- Shareholders may have difficulty in recovering their investment because of limitations on who can buy shares

- In Australia, a company pays the flat rate for company tax

- More expensive to set up and administer and greater reporting requirements

- Not normally suitable for smaller family farming businesses

## OTHER ARRANGEMENTS TO CONSIDER

### Self-Managed Super Fund (SMSF)

When thinking about the structure of your business, you might also like to consider setting up a self-managed super fund (SMSF). There are a number of advantages of a SMSF including significant tax advantages, especially for those with high taxable incomes and for long-term land holding as part of your succession plan. As you can imagine, establishing and operating an SMSF is very complex, so you will need professional legal and taxation advice.

## Advantages

- Income tax concessions

- Transfer of interests in farming land as contributions to an SMSF

- Members of SMSFs can now sign what is called a Binding Death Benefit Nomination, which ensures that any farming land held in the SMSF will, on the death of parents, pass down to the farmer's successor

- Land held in an SMSF is "outside" your will and is therefore protected from any will challenge as long as a valid Binding Death Benefit Nomination had been signed by the members of the SMSF

- For those with no farming successors, the SMSF can lease the land out on retirement with excellent taxation benefits

- No capital gains tax payable on any asset sold by a superannuation fund once its members have commenced to draw pensions from the fund

## Disadvantages

- Reduces the diversity of investments because failure of the farming business may also devalue the superannuation fund

- Prevents funds and assets from being accessed except as a result of death, retirement or disability

- Means that assets cannot be mortgaged and so the opportunity to borrow is restricted which will result in increased legal and accounting costs to operate the farming business

- Requires adherence to very strict legal and accounting requirements

## FARM MANAGEMENT DEPOSITS

Farm Management Deposits (FMDs) are a risk-management tool to help farmers deal with uneven income, which is common in agriculture because of natural disasters, climate and market variability.[35]

---

35  Australian Taxation Office - ATO (2014). *Farm management deposits scheme.*

FMDs are often gifted to a farming child as they are often perceived as being part of the farming assets. As tax is payable on the FMD in the year of date of death, tax for a deceased person would normally be paid out of residue.

Potentially, a farming child may receive the full cash value of an FMD, with the residuary beneficiaries being obliged to pick up the tax bill from the (often) meagre sum left in the residuary estate for non-farming children. To overcome that possibility, an FMD should always be bequeathed subject to the beneficiary paying income tax on the deposit.

## Advantages

- Set aside pre-tax income from primary production in years of high income, which you can draw on in years of low income

- Claim a tax deduction for FMDs you make in the income you made them provided the FMD is not withdrawn within 12 months

- Consolidating multiple FMDs will have no tax consequences provided you meet the requirements for merging deposits

- Can use FMDs as a tax-effective way to make contributions to superannuation funds

- There is a natural disaster exemption for early withdrawal of a deposit without losing tax benefits

## Disadvantages

- There is a cap on off-farm income (if a family member is working off the farm and earns more than $100,000 you may not be able to use FMDs)

- FMDs are currently capped at $400, 000

- Certain farm business structures are not eligible for FMDs (such as company)

- FMDs cannot be made by two or more people jointly or made on behalf of two or more people

- Trustees can only enter FMD agreements on behalf of a beneficiary who is entitled to a share of the income of the trust estate and is under a legal disability – for example, if they are a minor

- You need to have sufficient cash to make a deposit

# Life Interests

A life interest is a form of right, usually under a trust, which lasts only for the lifetime of the person benefiting from that right. A person with a life interest is known as a life tenant. A life interest ends when the life tenant dies.

If you sell your property to your farming child, you can preserve an interest in your home by using a life interest. This life would entitle you to use of the property throughout the remainder of your life. Your interest would be registered so that it cannot be taken away or disposed of without your consent. Your child would receive what is called "a remainder interest" which guarantees ownership, subject to the rights contained in your life interest.

Another use of life interest is where a husband leaves his share of the family farm to his children but leaves his wife a life interest in their home. This means that the surviving partner can continue to live in their own home and cannot have it sold without their consent. This a good way to protect the living arrangements of the wife while giving ownership and control to the farming child.

## Advantages

* Protects living arrangements and gives assurance that the property will not be sold without consent by the "life tenant"
* Allows for the ownership of assets by the next generation while protecting the exiting generation

## Disadvantages

* You cannot sell the property unless the "life tenant" consents or dies

# Vendor Terms Agreement

A vendor term agreement in relation to family farms is when a sibling may agree to purchase some land from the parents using a vendor term agreement. This would work well when there is a land title that is clear (not mortgaged) as the parents would still hold ownership of the title and the sibling would purchase the land at an agreed price and then have time to pay the amount off.

For example, the vendor term was for ten years and the land amount was $400,000, the sibling would pay a nominal amount of interest as well as some principle over the ten years, so that the amount owing might be $200,000.

At that stage, the sibling might go to the bank to finalise the purchase from the parents, paying the parents out fully, and using the land acquired through a vendor term agreement as security for the loan.

The benefit for the family is that they have been able to give the sibling some independent financial control over his or her destiny. The sibling has the incentive to work harder to pay off the debt to the parents and the sibling has also been able to use capital appreciation to increase the amount of capital, as long as the market for land has not gone down.

This process with the potential of capital plant purchases helps to promote the next generation of farming businesses, which is good for the local community and farming sector in general.

## Binding Agreements (Pre/Post Nuptial Agreements)

A binding financial agreement is an agreement between de facto, soon to be married or already married couples, which is made either before, during or after their relationship.

Types of binding financial agreements include:

- Pre-nuptial agreements
- Post-nuptial agreements
- Co-habitation agreements
- Separation agreements
- Divorce agreements

Basically, a binding financial agreement states how your assets, financial resources and liabilities will be divided if a relationship breaks down.

In family farming, a binding financial agreement can be an important way to protect farming assets if a marriage breaks down. You have surely seen situations where a marriage breaks down and the farming partner has to buy back his share of the farm from his former spouse, creating financial stress and issues in the family.

There are many people who scoff at these agreements and say they aren't worth the piece of paper they're written on and yes, there are instances where this has shown to be true. Even among lawyers, there is an increasingly strong view that the normal property settlement procedures of the Family Law Act are a fairer and easier means to follow in a divorce.

However, farming often involves multiple generations, a lot of assets and liabilities and complex business structures making a case for having some sort of financial agreement in place as marriage breakdown can actually spell disaster for a farming operation.

One thing to think about though is that there may be an impact on the non-farming spouse who feels emotionally disconnected from the business because they know that business is not a joint or marital asset.

Also it's important to think of a pre-nuptial agreement, not in terms of a couple thinking their marriage will fail but rather that they are planning for the continued success of their farming business.

And don't forget that marriage negates any previous wills. So if you don't have an up-to-date will, now is the time to get on to it but rewrite your will after marriage!

## Life & Disability Insurance

We cannot stress enough just how important it is to protect yourself and your family with life and disability insurance. We highly recommend that you have life insurance for each family member working on the farm as well as partners.

Ask yourself how your farming business would operate if you, your partner or another family member were:

- Killed unexpectedly

- Had an accident, became disabled and were no longer able to work

- Required full time care due to illness or disability

Any of these could happen. If your partner got a terminal illness, wouldn't you want to spend as much time with them as possible? If you have young children, wouldn't they need you more if the other parent died?

This is the harsh reality of life, whether you are a famer or not. Life is precarious and uncertain. Life and disability insurance can provide some peace of mind that if something bad happens, your family has some income to help them.

Just in case you're feeling complacent about getting insurance, let us share some scary facts from a report by Safe Work Australia about farming injuries and fatalities:[36]

- From 1 July 2003 to 30 June 2011, **356 workers died** while working on a farming property

- This is **17% of all worker fatalities** in Australia

- Nearly **one-third** of the worker fatalities on farms were workers aged **65 years or over**

- Incidents involving vehicles accounted for 71% of fatalities on farms:
    - **Tractors** were involved in **93** (26%) farm deaths
    - **Light vehicles** were involved in **28** (8%)
    - **Quad bikes** were involved in **27** (8%)

- Between 2009 and 2010, **17, 400 agriculture workers had incurred a work-related injury** or illness in the previous 12 months - this equates to 56.4 injuries per 1000 workers

In case you hadn't realised, farming is one of the most dangerous jobs in Australia.

Now if that doesn't motivate you, here are some statistics about death, illness and disability in Australia:[37]

---

36  Safe Work Australia, (2014). *Work-related injuries and fatalities on Australian farms - Safe Work Australia.*

37  Australian Network of Disability, (2014). *Disability Statistics.* Australian Institute of Health & Welfare (AIHW), (2014). *Leading types of ill health (AIHW).*

- In 2011, there **were 43,221 deaths** from **cancer** in Australia, accounting for 3 in 10 deaths

- In 2007, about **1 in 28** living Australians had been diagnosed with cancer at some time in the previous 26 years

- In 2011–12, an estimated **585,900** Australians had **coronary heart disease**

- In 2011, an estimated **69,900** people aged 25 and over had **a heart attack**

- **45%** of Australians aged 16–85 have experienced a **mental disorder** sometime in their lifetime (equating to 7.3 million people)

- An estimated **1 in 5** (20%) of the population aged 16–85 (equating to 3.2 million people) had experienced a **common mental disorder** in the previous 12 months

- **3.4 million** (15%) Australians have a **physical disability**

- Over **4 million** (about 1 in 5) Australians have a **disability**

- **2.1 million** Australians of working age (15 – 64 years) have a **disability**

# Our Insurance Story

When we were first married, we didn't have any life or disability insurance. After the birth of our son, Spencer, we realised that if something happened to either of us, we needed to provide for the surviving spouse and our children.

**Nick:** *I had tried to get insurance in the past when I was farming with my brother Chris but we didn't end up getting insurance because we were trying to insure our whole operation and the premium was ridiculous.*

*When I had my son, Spencer, I realised I needed to rethink my insurance needs. Rather than insuring our whole farming income, Ayesha and I both got death, disability and serious illness insurance to the value of $500,000 each.*

*The premium was affordable at less than $1,000 dollars each per year and gives me the assurance that Ayesha and the kids will be okay if something happens to me.*

**Ayesha:** *I was scared that if Nick died, it would take me a long time to liquidate the farmland and machinery. In the meantime, I would have to pay mortgage and machinery repayments, school fees, taxes, rates, insurance, vehicle registrations and other living expenses. I realised that we needed to have life insurance.*

*I then wondered what would happen if Nick was injured on the farm or got a serious illness. How would we survive? I realised we also needed disability and serious illness insurance.*

*Then I got to thinking, what happens if I get ill? I would need Nick to stay at home and care for me and the children. He would not be able to farm fulltime. Or if I died, the kids would need Nick more as he would be their fulltime carer. So, I decided to get insurance for myself as well.*

*At the same time, Nick and I also sorted out our wills to ensure our wishes were written down and legally documented. We discussed who would have the children if we died and asked family friends if they would (which they agreed to). I also had to consider my father in the equation as he lives with us and we would not like him to be destitute if we both died.*

*I hope that we will not have to use this insurance but I have the peace of mind that if something bad happened, we would have the financial security provided by our insurance to help manage the situation.*

*Phew, you did it. You made it through the most boring chapter in this book. Now let's have a look at a case study where the father dies, the mother is still alive and the son is farming. After that, we will explore how we can develop the next generation of farming leaders.*

# Case Study 12:

# Dad Dies, Mum Still Alive, Son Farming

*" I'd only been farming a few years with my dad when he died. Dad's will stipulated that Mum have a life interest in the land and that I had to give a share of the farm to my siblings upon her death. We ended up changing all that so that I have the land and my siblings will still get their fair share. "*

Sometimes when the father dies before his wife, he can leave a life interest in the farm so that her needs for a house and security are taken care of but that the children still get what they need as well.

### Tim's Story

My dad, Colin McBride, was a farmer his whole life. He lived on the farm with his wife of 25 years, Betty. We'd farmed together for the last four years, since I finished school. When Dad died, his will stipulated that I had use of the small farm and Mum was given a life interest in the land.

So as stipulated in Dad's will, I signed an agreement stating that I will give a share of the farm to my brother and sister when my Mum passes away. Thankfully, the share I have to give my siblings takes into account the value of the education they have received that was paid for by the farm.

Mum owned the land jointly with Dad and after his death, I originally leased it back from her but we later decided, after getting some advice, that Mum would transfer the ownership of the land to me. She did this on the proviso that I understood that she would leave everything else to my brother and sister.

This has allowed me to develop the farm without the burden of future debt that would have been created to pay out my siblings. This also allowed Mum to have her own security and peace of mind that the other two kids would be treated fairly.

## THE LESSONS

- A life share is one option of providing for the surviving partner
- The needs of the surviving partner need to be addressed to ensure that they have income and housing for the rest of their lives
- The siblings share in the assets took into consideration the value of the their education which was paid for by the farm
- Establish an asset value base that takes into consideration the cost of the education of the off-farm siblings paid for by the farm during the time the son was working on the farm with his father
- You need to have life insurance for the working partners (such as the father and son)

# How Do You Develop the Next Generation?

# Chapter 13:

# How Do You Develop the Next Generation?

*"It takes time and experience to become a leader in business. In family farming, the younger generation needs opportunities to develop their leadership and business management skills."*

## Nick Shady

When you really look at a farming enterprise, you realise just how much one family has to know in order to run a successful business. It is imperative that the next generation runs the farm as a business if it is going survive and hopefully thrive in the future.

## WHAT A LEADER & WHY DO WE NEED THEM?

Leadership is the ability to set an objective, explore alternatives, take action and change course as appropriate.

Just like any business or organisation, family farming needs skilled leaders to ensure viability and growth. Leadership is important in family farming for a number of reasons:

- A family farm is a complex business that requires leadership and management skills to ensure that it remains viable into the future and can provide financially for family members.

- By its very nature, family farming has a high risk of conflict and therefore needs good leaders to manage and minimise conflict. People are by nature emotional and working and living with family brings its own unique set of problems.

- It involves motivating, inspiring and empowering other family members to contribute to the success of the farming operation.

Family farms need leadership to survive. In the corporate world, a new manager can be hired easily enough. In farming, leadership naturally falls to the successor/s. At its worst, poor leadership can lead to family conflict and relationship breakdowns, bad financial situations and possibly the loss of the farm and other assets.

People are not necessarily born business leaders. They need training, mentoring and guidance.

## EXPERTISE REQUIRED FOR FARMING LEADERS

Farming is a complex business. Just have a look at some of the things you need to know to successfully manage a farm business:

- Finance
- Accounting
- Taxation
- Economics
- Health & safety
- Employment laws
- Staff management
- Insurance
- Commodity markets
- Contract law
- Grain & livestock marketing
- Agronomy
- Business processes
- Business structures
- Superannuation
- Retirement strategies
- Asset management

- Communication & mediation
- Legislative requirements
- Management & leadership

We hope that when you look at the list above you give yourself a pat on the back for mastering at least some of these. This list highlights just how much you need to learn and experience in order to take on the management of the farm. One person doesn't have to know all these things but someone in the business needs to cover the different areas.

## PERSONAL QUALITIES OF A GOOD LEADER

In addition to skills, experience and knowledge, a good leader also needs to have certain qualities.

A good leader is:

- Trustworthy
- Confident
- Intuitive
- Visionary
- Risk tolerant
- Flexible
- Proactive
- Empathetic
- Able to develop good relationships
- Can be charismatic
- Emotionally intelligent

While many of these qualities are inborn, good leaders can develop behaviours that might offset the absence of these characteristics. For example, some leaders are not very risk tolerant however, they can take actions that demonstrate the opposite because they know that it is in the best interests of the farming operation.

## DEVELOPING THE NEXT GENERATION OF LEADERS

Now more than ever, the farming sector needs strong leaders to ensure that family farming continues into the future. Farming families are the key to keeping small country towns alive, providing food to feed our nation and in supporting the Australian economy.

How do we develop the leadership and management skills of the next generation? We need to do it in a systematic and conscious manner. There are a number of ways to do this, including:

- Training & development planning for successors

- Leadership & business mentoring

- Self-education

- Education & training

### Training & Development Plan for Successors

In your succession plan, make sure you include a training and development plan. You really need to build up the next generation's skills before they take on the full ownership and management of the business.

Your training and development plan outlines the skills and knowledge required by the successor and compares these with their current skills. Identify any gaps that need to be addressed and make sure you have strategies in place to build up their skills in these areas.

Here are some questions to consider when developing a training and development plan for each successor:

- What is the current ability, educational and skill limitations?

- For which business functions or operational systems are they currently responsible?

- What kind of development is necessary to improve their skills and abilities?

- What kinds of management skills and abilities are necessary to manage future business operations?

- What are their strengths?

- What are their weaknesses?
- Where are their skill gaps?
- What do they most enjoy and what do they dislike?

## Leadership & Business Mentoring

Informal or formal mentoring provides an invaluable resource for developing leadership and business skills. Find someone you can learn from and ask them to mentor you. You can also learn from someone even if you don't have a personal relationship with them by watching what they do and how they do it, learning from their actions and outcomes. The opportunity to learn from the experience of another person is priceless.

## Self-Education

There is a need for lifelong learning in any industry and farming is no different. You need to be continually learning. Here are some ways to increase your knowledge and skills:

- Read books, newspapers, magazines
- Participate in industry forums
- Subscribe to online newsletters
- Go to seminars
- Look up information online
- Speak to people who know more than you on a particular topic
- Ask questions of your team of advisors

## Education & Training

There are numerous opportunities for education and training available to farmers to increase their knowledge and skills and can include:

- TAFE Course
- University Course
- Online Courses

- Vocation Courses

The training required will depend on the individual needs of your business. Keep your eye out for educational opportunities and encourage everyone in the business to take up these opportunities. You may find that there are many courses that are provided at low cost or with funding from the government. You don't necessarily have to spend a fortune to develop your skills.

## Building Relationships with Professional Services

The next generation of leaders also needs to have good relationships with the professional services team that helps you run your business. Include the younger generation in meetings with your accountant, solicitor, bank manager, agronomist and other professionals that service your business. This will help them understand the complexities of your farming enterprise while building important relationships for the future.

## Harnessing Cross Generational Knowledge

There is a lot of knowledge capital locked up in the older generation and there is also a lot of new information that the next generation can bring to the table. Between the two generations, there is an opportunity for family farming to become stronger, more efficient and more prosperous.

In order for the successor generation to learn, the senior generation needs to delegate some responsibility, allowing the successor to make decisions and suffer the consequences of any mistakes, though the senior generation should definitely provide advice if asked or if they see a major catastrophe looming.

## Nick's Story

I went to a private school in Ballarat. I was the youngest in my year and I didn't do very well at school. I was too busy mucking around to pay much attention to my studies. When I worked for the National Australia Bank, I realised that I wasn't stupid (immature, yes) and that I could learn new skills that I would later utilise on the farm.

I enjoy learning and applying new skills. I never really thought about getting any qualifications once I was back working with my family on the farm. I was always learning informally about how to manage the farm finances, set up a self-managed super fund, manage a share portfolio and buy off-farm assets.

When I got married to Ayesha, I started to think about other opportunities for my future. With her encouragement and support, I applied to do a Masters of Business Management (MBA) at the University of Ballarat (now Federation University).

I did very well in my studies and I learned a lot. The experience gave me more confidence in myself. I also realised just how useful good business practices and skills are to farming businesses.

Since finishing my MBA a couple of years ago, I've also studied occupational health and safety and real estate. All the skills and knowledge I have acquired is used in my business to make it as successful as possible.

---

*Most farmers don't see themselves as leaders but if you run a business, and especially if you have a team working with you, then you need to learn to be a leader. Now let's have a look at a case study about expanding the farm operations so that it can support more than one family. After that, we will explore knowing when it is time for the older generation to transition control and assets.*

---

# Case Study 13:

# Expanding the Farm for Future Independence

*" I thought we had everything sorted. We had our plan in place and we grew our farm so that it would support all of us. But now, I feel like I got ripped off in the deal and I don't know what will happen to my parents' land when they die. We were trying to avoid the succession planning disasters we had seen in other families but now all we've done is create a lot of tension and stress."*

Expanding the farm operations with the clear goal of supporting the retiring generation and the successor families has worked for a number of family farms. These days, it can be hard for a single farming entity to generate enough income to support say four separate families. Through growing the farm business, each individual family unit can have a decent income and a secure financial future. However, tensions can arise when you break up these assets and one person feels like they haven't been treated fairly in the deal.

### Chris & Brian's Story

Gavin Clements and his two sons, Chris and Brian, have worked together for 20 years. During that time, they have had expanded their land holdings threefold. Ownership was split three ways – Gavin and wife Deirdre, Chris and Brian. They were each able to own a third because of their focus on expanding the farm.

Part of the reason they structured their business this way originally was so that they could split the farming business to create financial independence when the sons married and had children of their own.

Now that Chris and Brian are both married, and Chris and his wife Melissa are expecting their first child, they have split up the farming entity so that each family has their own farming operation. They are independent with regards to land ownership. They share plant equipment and help each other out as needed.

Unfortunately, Chris feels like Brian got the better deal in the asset break up. Chris thinks the land he got is not as good as Brian's and it doesn't yield as much per acre. The house on the property is very old and Brian's wife wants to renovate it to make it more liveable before their baby arrives.

There is quite a lot of tension between the brothers because of this. There is also the issue about who will inherit the parents' share when Gavin and Deirdre pass away. This has not been addressed and each brother feels like they should get it.

Assuming it is left equally to both brothers, they would have to sell it and split the profits or one could lease half of it from the other or one brother would have to buy it outright from the other. The uncertainty is putting stress on the brothers' relationship.

## THE LESSONS

- Expand your farming business so that it can sustain all family members

- Structure your farming business so that it can be split up to create autonomy and financial security for each family unit

- Reduce the risk of resentment and disharmony by having a plan in place for when adult children marry and have a family of their own

- Try to ensure that the division of assets is as fair as possible

- An estate plan needs to be in place and communicated clearly to reduce the stress caused by uncertainty

- If grandchildren want to farm, they can farm with their parents and not under their uncles or grandparents

# How Do You Know It's Time to Transition?

# Chapter 14:

# How Do You Know It's Time to Transition?

*"I thought I wanted to retire. So we handed over the farm operations to our son and moved to the beach but I didn't know what to do with myself. I was bored. I was used to working every day. My wife got sick of having me underfoot and we had no connections in the community. I feel like I made a terrible mistake."*

### Retired Farmer

Farmers are different from other types of workers. They are more emotionally attached to their work and the farm is their primary investment. Most don't expect to retire and stop farming altogether. They are more likely to think of reducing their hours or the scope of their operations. Often, there is also a strong desire to keep the farm in the family.

So, how do you know when to pass on the operation to the next generation?

Not sure if you are ready to hand transition out of the family farming business?

Reflect on these questions to get some insight into your readiness to transition out of your farming business:

- Is your business transition ready?

- Are you ready to retire?

- Are there alternatives to retirement?

- Is your successor ready to take control?

These questions are explored in further detail below. Answer these questions honestly and then discuss them with your spouse and the rest of your family.

## IS YOUR BUSINESS TRANSITION READY?

- Is your business positioned for growth and development beyond the current owner?

- Do you have a plan for achieving your retirement objectives?

- Are you, your family, your associates, your suppliers, your customers and your banker certain that your business will continue through a generational transfer?

- Do you have a financial plan in place for your business in case you don't wake up tomorrow?

- Do you have a trusted resource to guide financial decisions consistent with your wants and needs?

- What have you done about succession planning?

## ARE YOU READY TO RETIRE?

- Will I continue to work in the business or in a completely new venture?

- Will I do volunteer work or pursue hobbies?

- Assuming that a person can only play so much, what else will I do?

- As I prepare for retirement, how do I want to develop my business?

## WHAT ARE YOUR ALTERNATIVES TO RETIREMENT?

- Would you like to continue to work part-time on the farm?

- Would you like to provide coaching and advice to the successor?

- Would you like to give up the physical side of farming?

- Do you still want to live on the farm and be available to help the successor?

- Do you still need to earn an income because you don't have enough money to retire?

- Would you consider working part-time for another local farmer who needs seasonal help?

## IS THE SUCCESSOR READY TO TAKE CONTROL?

- Is your successor ready for the responsibility?

- Do they have the skills and experience to take over?

- Have you already given them responsibilities and allowed them to make mistakes?

## THE ADVANTAGES & DISADVANTAGES OF RETIRING

We all appreciate time away from work and need time to recharge our batteries and renew our enthusiasm. Though retirement sounds like a wonderful extended vacation, free time may not have the same value if there is no work to return to.

You've probably met farmers that are happily retired but you might also know farmers who have retired and regretted it. So, before you do anything drastic like move down the coast, have a look at the pros and cons of retiring and discuss them with your family.

### Advantages

The biggest advantage of retirement is that you have more time for the things you love. Some of these might include more time for:

- Grandchildren

- Hobbies

- Spouse (this can be a disadvantage for some couples!)

- Fitness

- Travel

- Relaxing

- Learning a new skill

- Contributing to your local community and volunteering

- Joining boards and committees

## Disadvantages

- Boredom – too much time on your hands and not enough to do

- Loss of community if moving to a new town

- Too much time with your spouse

- No income coming in

- No routine

- Lack of motivation because you have nothing you absolutely have to do

Regardless of when you decide to retire and transition out of the business, you need to have a clearly defined exit strategy. You need to develop a succession plan and have enough money for the enjoyment of your retirement.

*Retiring from farming after a lifetime on the land is a big deal and not an easy decision but hopefully this chapter has given you some clarity. Next we will share a case study where the older generation are obsessed with leaving a debt free farm and how that can impact the financial viability of the business for the next generation. After the case study, we get to a really tough topic – leaving the family farm when there seems to be no other choice.*

# Case Study 14:

# Leaving a Debt Free Farm

*" I feel trapped. I've worked on the farm for 20 years for the smallest of wages. Our small farm can't support two families. I want to buy more land but my parents are scared to go into debt. They don't mind if I borrow money but I don't have any collateral so I can't get a loan."*

Small farms today cannot always provide financially for all family members. Most successful farming families have had to expand their farming operations to ensure their continued economic viability.

There is good debt and bad debt and you need to know the difference between the two. If you take on debt that will increase your income and your asset base and you can service the load, then it's a good debt to have.

### Jane's Story

I have farmed alongside my parents for nearly twenty years. I only get paid a small wage and I work six days a week. The farm is too small to support both families and things are pretty tight.

My parents do not want to borrow against the farm to expand the farming operation and its land holdings. While they flatly refuse to borrow money to buy more land, they don't object to me borrowing money but with no assets of my own to use as collateral and only a small income, there is no way I can get a loan.

I feel trapped. I'm in my late 30s with a young family. I have no skills or experience outside of farming and I have no assets. Basically, I'm stuck. And yet, my siblings consider me lucky because one day I might eventually inherit the farm.

While I can understand my parents' strong desire to leave a debt free farm, it means we can't expand our operations to create a better income for both families.

Sometimes I wonder if I would have been better off working as a labourer on another family farm. Am I wasting my life on the farm, waiting for that day when I inherit the farm and struggling to survive in the meantime?

## THE LESSONS

- Security is a major issue for parents and children alike

- Leaving a debt free farm shouldn't be achieved at the expense of creating a sustainable enterprise that can support all family members

- Inheriting a debt free farm in 20 years can't make up for living hand to mouth in the meantime

- Discuss the parents' exit plan early so that everyone has the same understanding and expectations

- Consider vendor finance so that you can own the land and have financial independence

# If All Else Fails, Should You Leave the Farm?

# Chapter 15:

# If All Else Fails, Should You Leave the Farm?

*"In the end, I just had to give up my dream of running the family farm. It was heartbreaking but I felt like I had no other choice. I miss the farm every day."*

### Former Farmer

This is not a chapter we want to write but it's important to know that if you've tried your hardest and you still don't have a succession plan that everyone is happy with, what next?

There comes a point where your needs and those of the rest of your family just might not meet. You need one thing, they want another. Even with compromise on both sides, there still might not be enough of what you need and want to make it work.

The priority in all of this is to keep relationships civil and hopefully loving while creating the life you want for yourself and your immediate family.

If you can't get a succession plan developed and implemented due to family conflict or you aren't happy with the outcome of the plan, here are your options:

1. **Live with the situation** as is with either no formal succession plan or one you're not happy with

2. Leave the family farm and **start your own** farming enterprise

3. Leave farming altogether and **get a job or start a business**

Look at these three options and think about these questions:

- Which one can you live with?

- Which one would make you happier?

- Which one will make you feel resentful and angry?
- Which one would create the least amount of tension and stress in your family relationships?
- What does your spouse think?

At the end of the day, as we've said before in this book, life is a precious gift. Do not squander it being miserable. If you're not happy, do something about it.

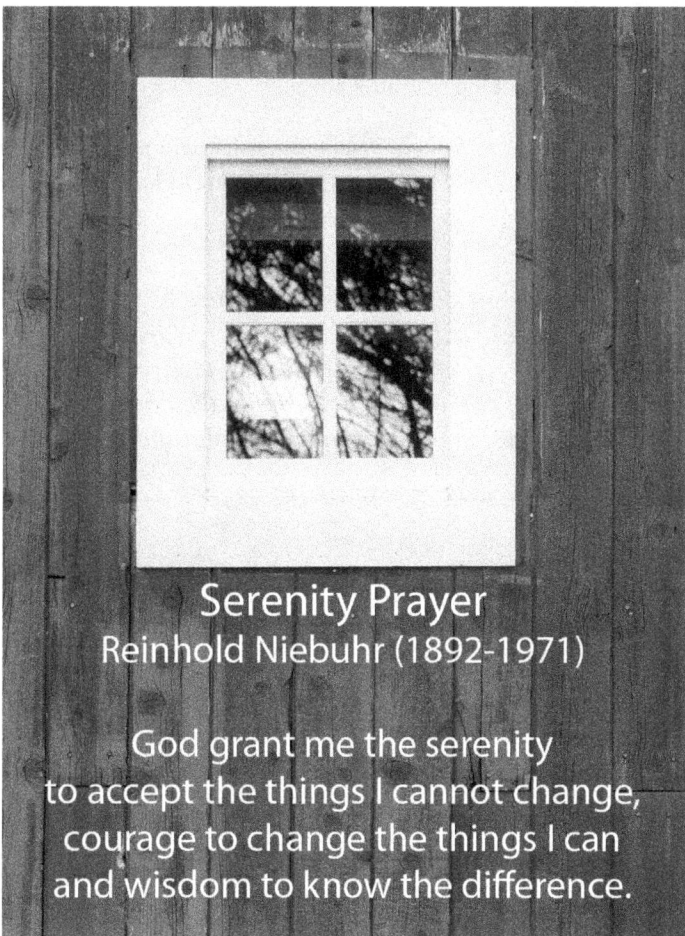

## Serenity Prayer
### Reinhold Niebuhr (1892-1971)

God grant me the serenity
to accept the things I cannot change,
courage to change the things I can
and wisdom to know the difference.

If you choose to stay with a less than ideal succession plan or no plan at all, accept it as your current reality. At least you know what you're getting yourself into. Make the most of it. And you can always try to develop a better succession plan later (but don't hold your breath waiting for this to happen).

If you want to leave the family farm and start your own farm, go for it! Yes, you'll probably have a lot of debt but at least you will be independent and in charge of your own destiny.

If you decide to leave farming and get a job, see what it's like. You may love the regular income and hours. You may hate it. You may even decide to start your own business in something new altogether.

Whatever you choose, make sure you choose what will make you the happiest. Be true to yourself and your own needs, while being as kind as possible to other family members.

*Okay, this was a short chapter with some tough love. Next we share a case study about a son and his family leaving the farming business even though he would have preferred to have kept farming if possible. Now we are in the home stretch with just the conclusion to go after this!*

# Case Study 15:

# Son Decides to Leave Farming

*" I'm not happy about leaving the farm. I felt like I had no choice. I couldn't live with the fighting any more. I wished Dad would change but he's a stubborn old man. He wouldn't even entertain the idea of succession planning. He just wants to control everything and everyone. I had to leave for my own sanity and the future of my family. "*

When the two generations can't agree to develop a succession plan, the younger generation doesn't like the lack of security and worries about their financial future.

Sometimes, when a succession plan can't be developed and implemented, the only option for the next generation is to leave the farm altogether. For many, this is a last resort that is heartbreaking.

### Billy & Annabel's Story

Billy and Annabel have been married for five years. They have two young children. They farmed with Billy's mum and dad. The farm hadn't turned over much of profit for the last eight years due to drought and bad business decisions.

There was a lot of conflict between Billy and his dad because Billy had lots of ideas on how to turn the farming business around and start making a profit but Billy's dad is as stubborn as an old bull that's been put out to pasture. He won't budge and he doesn't like new ideas. He's been farming for 40 years and he thinks he knows everything.

Annabel was fed up with the whole situation. Her husband was unhappy and complained about his dad all the time. They had no money and no financial security. She encouraged Billy to start the succession planning process with his dad and off-farm siblings but his dad wouldn't even talk about succession planning.

After many arguments and an increasing level of family conflict, Billy and Annabel realised that the only way forward was for them to leave the family farm. This made them both sad but they just couldn't live with the increasing level of conflict while waiting for Billy's dad to retire (if indeed he ever did). They were also stressed about their financial future.

So they moved off the farm and Billy got a job in a local timber mill. He was soon promoted to manager of the maintenance department because he was so good at fixing machinery (all those years fixing farm machinery paid off).

He's earning a good income and his wife is a lot happier. He is on speaking terms with the rest of his family, though his Dad still doesn't understand why he left the farm. Billy misses the farm and still dreams of buying his own one day.

## THE LESSONS

- It takes commitment from everyone involved in the farming business to get a succession plan in place – it's not something one member can do on their own (especially if you're not the main owner of the farming enterprise)

- No matter how hard you try, sometimes you just have to call it quits and cut your losses

- Better to know now that wait until you're 60, with no assets of your own and no retirement fund

# Conclusion:

# Final Thoughts

*" We can't solve problems by using the same kind of thinking we used when we created them. "*

*Albert Einstein*

We hope that you have enjoyed reading this book and you've got some great ideas and inspiration to help you in your succession planning process. As you have seen, succession planning is a journey for your whole family – hopefully, one that will make your family stronger, more harmonious and more prosperous.

It's far easier to read and talk about succession planning than it is to put into action. Succession planning requires family members with differing needs, expectations and personalities to meet in the spirit of cooperation and compromise for the good of the whole family and the farming business. You will need to negotiate the how, what and when of transitioning the farm to the next generation.

If you commit to the succession planning process now rather than waiting for disaster to strike, your family and your business will be in a much stronger position. Parents can begin letting go, allowing adult children to make more decisions and assume more responsibility. Children become more assertive, often rising to new levels of responsibility and accountability.

In conclusion, we urge you to:

- **Get started** with your succession planning process
- Gather a **team of experts** to help guide you on the journey
- **Review** your succession plan regularly
- Ensure you have an **estate plan** in place that works with your succession plan
- **Communicate** with your family about what you want and need

- **Listen** to other family members about their issues and concerns

We wish you all the best in your family farming business and hope that you are able to create a succession plan that pleases as many people in your family as possible with as little conflict as possible.

With best wishes,

*Nick Shady & Ayesha Hilton*

# About the Authors

# Nick Shady

Nick Shady is a fourth-generation farmer who is also an international author, speaker, business owner, volunteer counsellor and farm management expert.

For nearly thirty years, Nick has been involved with his family's farming business in rural Victoria, Australia. With his brother, Chris Shady, Nick turned the family farm from 2,000 acres to just over 5,500 acres, turning over millions of dollars per annum.

In 2019 Nick sold his last remaining farming block, and still continues share farming and contracting in his local area.

Nick is passionate about working with family farm businesses so they can be more successful, remain efficient, profitable, self-managed and most importantly stay together amidst changes in the agricultural industry. He teaches how family farms can work the land in a sustainable and profitable manner, thereby maintaining and strengthening rural communities.

In his late thirties, Nick attended university for the first time and gained a Master's in Business Administration. He brings his business administration skills to his consulting business where he works with agricultural businesses and service providers, along with farming families. His considerable experience in the agri-business sector gives Nick tremendous scope and hands on experience, often sought by businesses that are having issues with marketing or business expansion.

Nick is very active in his local community has served in various executive roles for the local district including the Beaufort & Skipton Health Service Foundation, Beaufort Community Bank, Skipton Recreation Reserve, Sports Central Ballarat, the Skipton Football & Netball Club and is a member of the Stockyard Hill Windfarm Reference committee.

Nick was the founding chairperson of the Friends of the RSL – Skipton Branch. Nick saw the need for change with the help of the Ex RSL local branch members, to continue the tradition and presence for returned services people in the area. Nick worked with the Victorian RSL to initiate Australia's first Friends of the RSL for communities who have a small number of returned service people or none at all, who still wanted to have an RSL presence. The resulting success of this initiative has seen the model utilised around the country.

Nick is also a passionate about farmer mental health and works to reduce the suicide rate and negative health issues that face farmers and the crippling effects they can have on families and the local community.

He has travelled extensively to over 10 countries including the United States of America, England, France, Germany, Belgium, South Africa, Ireland and New Zealand just to name a few.

Find out more about Nick at:

www.nickshady.com

# Ayesha Hilton

Ayesha is an Amazon Bestselling author, mother of two, spiritual adventurer and avid learner. She shares her contagious enthusiasm, caring nature and love of learning and teaching through her transformational coaching and training to women around the world.

With eclectic talents and interests, Ayesha has narrowed her top three passions to books, business and personal growth.

She's found that being in business forces you to grow exponentially as a woman and a leader (and yes there are sometimes growing pains).

Ayesha has published a number of other books, as well as colouring books for adults, and journals. She is also a contributing author of the Amazon bestseller anthologies.

With a love of travel that started at an early age, Ayesha has travelled, trained and worked in seven countries including the United States of America, Nepal, Laos, Burma, and Papua New Guinea.

She also lived for several years in Chiang Mai, Thailand, where she was a volunteer with Australian Volunteers International working with Thai sex workers and Burmese refugees. Ayesha was brought up Buddhist and as a child lived in Northern India where she has a strong connection to the home base of the Dalai Lama.

Ayesha believes that gratitude is the key to creating the best life possible and she knows just how blessed she is. Ayesha lives in rural Victoria, Australia, with her two children Grace and Spencer, along with Ayesha's father, known affectionately as Grandpa, and their cat Pippa.

Find out more about Ayesha at:

www.ayeshahilton.com

www.facebook.com/ayeshahiltonpage

# Recommended Resources

We have compiled a list of resources that may be of interest to you in your succession planning process.

## COUNSELLING/MENTAL HEALTH/SUICIDE PREVENTION

*Farming is a stressful business. If you're feeling depressed, stressed, suicidal or just need someone to talk to, please reach out and get support.*

**Survivors of Suicide**

www.surivorsofsuicide.com.au

**beyondblue**
Support Service: 1300 22 4636
www.beyondblue.org.au

**Lifeline**
13 11 14
www.lifeline.org.au/Get-Help/

**Suicide Call Back Service**
1300 659 467
www.suicidecallbackservice.org.au

**SANE Australia Helpline**
1800 18 SANE (7263)
www.sane.org

**Mental Illness Fellowship North Queensland Inc.**
We are a specialist mental health services provider in the North Queensland region – from Sarina in the south, Mt Isa and the border in the west and Torres Strait Islands in the north. We have offices in Townsville, Cairns and Mackay.

www.mifnq.org.au

**CORES (Community Response to Eliminating Suicide) Program**
Phone: (03) 6491 1552
www.cores.org.au

## RURAL FINANCIAL COUNSELLING SERVICES

There are state based Rural Financial Counselling Services that provide advice on succession planning processes. Contact your local state service.

- Western Australia www.rfcswa.com.au

- Victoria and Tasmania www.ruralfinancialcounselling.org.au

- New South Wales Central www.rfcs-cw.com.au

- New South Wales Southern www.rfcsnsw-sr.com.au

- Queensland Central Southern Region www.rfcsqcsr.com.au

- Queensland South Western Region www.rfcsqsw.org.au

- South Australia www.ruralbusinesssupport.org.au

- Federal Government website www.agriculture.gov.au

## SUCCESSION PLANNING

You may already have a team of professionals to help you with your succession plan. Ask your lawyer, accountant or banker for referrals to someone local to you or have a look at this list of professionals to help you on your succession planning journey.

### MOR
This is who we personally use for all our accountancy needs. The team at MOR have supported and advised us well over the years and we even invited our accountant, Paul, to our wedding.

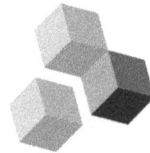

### Alan Blackburn & Associates Consulting

Geelong based consulting firm specialising in supporting farming clients.

Phone: (03)52296196 | www.farmconsultant.com.au

### Bedbrook Johnston & Williams (BJW)

BJW provides services to agricultural enterprises in the South West land division of Western Australia including areas from Geraldton to Esperance.

www.bjw.net.au

### Auswild & Broad

Auswild and Broad is an accounting firm located in the Riverina area of New South Wales. Head office is in Temora.

Phone (02) 6978 0077 | www.auswildbroad.com.au

### ANZ Banking

Speak to your local Agribusiness manager to get a referral to their team of farm succession experts.

www.anz.com.au

### Bicknells Accountants

Based in Ballarat, Victoria, Bicknells Accountants can provide your business with the right succession advice for your circumstances.

Phone: (03) 53315440 | www.bicknell.com.au

### Cappelo Rowe Lawyers

Cappelo Rowe are a law firm originally founded in Griffith NSW, they provide succession planning advice.

Phone: (02)69623433 | www.cappellorowe.com.au

### Cinque Oakley Senior (COS) Lawyers

Based in Ballarat, COS Lawyers provide a range of services to rural clients. We use Dean Cinque and his team for our personal and business legal requirements.

Phone: (03) 5331 5466 | www.coslawyers.com.au

### Consult Ag

Consult Ag are a Western Australian agricultural consultant firm whose main objective is to work closely with farmers to help achieve their personal, financial and family goals.

Phone: (08) 6253 2000 | www.consultag.com.au

### Degaris Lawyers

Based at Mount Gambier, Degaris Lawyers service the Limestone Coast area in South Australia, helping agricultural clients create and implement their succession plans.

Phone: (08) 8723 1144 | www.degarislawyers.com.au

### Don Naughton Consulting

Based in Bendigo, Victoria, Don Naughton Consulting helps farming families create a culture of respect in the family to help with succession planning.

Phone: (03) 54396305 | www.naunton.com.au

### Farmanco

Farmanco are consultants on succession planning, financial advice and farm business building and based in Western Australia.

www.farmanco.com.au

### Farm Plan Plus

FPP Accountants are based in Gunnedah, NSW. They guide farmers with the help of other professionals to implement a succession plan.

Phone: (02) 6742 6600 | www.fppaccountants.com.au

### Fleming Muntz

Solicitors with experience in farm succession planning, servicing Southern New South Wales and North-Eastern Victoria.

Phone: (02) 6021 2222 | www.flemingmuntz.com.au

### Goulburn Murray Hume AgCare

Goulburn Murray Hume Agcare Ltd are rural financial counsellors, helping clients in the Goulburn Valley and North East Victoria area.

Phone: 1300 834 775 | www.gmhagcare.org.au

### Harwood Andrews Lawyers

Based in Victoria, Harwood Andrews Lawyers help their rural clients to plan and implement their farm succession plans. Talk to your closest office for further details.

www.harwoodandrews.com.au

### High Resolutions

High Resolutions is a group of farm facilitators that help farming families get on their path to succession planning.

www.highresolutions.com.au

### Meridian Agriculture

Meridian Agriculture, (formally MSA) specialises in all aspects of farm business management.

Phone: (03) 53416100 | www.meridian-ag.com.au

### Mulcahy & Co

Mulcahy & Co is an accountancy firm located in Ballarat, Victoria. They provide advice for rural clients on farm succession issues.

Phone: (03) 53307200 | www.mulcahy.com.au

### NAB

NAB have specialist Farm Succession Planners on their team to help you with all your needs. Contact your Agribusiness Manager for more details.

www.nab.com.au

### Next Rural

Next Rural is a Sydney based specialised farm succession firm, they service clients Australia wide.

Phone: 1800 708495 | www.nextrural.com.au

### Pacer Legal

Pacer Legal are lawyers located in Perth, Geraldton and Karratha in Western Australia. They work with rural clients to support their businesses and deal with farm succession issues.

www.pacerlegal.com.au

### Proagtive

Specialist succession planners headed by Isobel Knight. Proagtive services farming families Australia wide with their own philosophy of how to have an ongoing succession plan.

Phone: 0448 461463 | www.proagtive.com.au

### Rabobank

Rabobank have their own farm succession planners that can work with families to get the right succession plan. Contact your local Agribusiness Manager for further details.

www.rabobank.com.au

### RSM Bird Cameron

An accountancy firm that has experience providing succession planning services to clients around Australia. RSM Bird Cameron has a national network of 28 offices. We personally know Bill Beard from the Ballarat office (you can give him a call on 03 5330 5800).

www.rsmi.com.au

### RMS Agricultural Consultants

Rural Management Strategies is a professional agricultural consultancy firm with offices based in Cootamundra and Wagga Wagga.

Phone: (02) 6942 3666 | www.rmsag.com.au

### Rural Directions Pty Ltd

Based at Clare and Freeling in South Australia, Rural Directions specialises in developing a positive succession outcome for your family.

Phone: (08) 88414500 |www.ruraldirections.com

### Rural Finance

Contact your nearest Agribusiness Relationship Manager to organise a discussion about your farm succession planning needs.

www.ruralfinance.com.au

### Vanguard Business Services

Based in Dubbo, New South Wales, Vanguard Business Services works with farming families to develop a no fuss succession plan.

Phone: (02) 6885 1925 | www.vbs.net.au

### Westpac Business

Westpac recommends you contact your Agribusiness Manager to get an Agribusiness Financial Planner to discuss your farm succession needs.

www.westpac.com.au

# PRIMARY & SECONDARY EDUCATION

BALLARAT GRAMMAR

Learning to Thrive
Engaged in the World

**Educating generations of your most precious assets.**

Three generations of the Macdonald Family, Darra, Meredith.

BALLARAT AND QUEEN'S ANGLICAN GRAMMAR SCHOOL

201 Forest Street, Wendouree Victoria 3355
p +61 (0)3 5338 0700    www.bgs.vic.edu.au

with hard work and good instruction anything is possible...
www.clarendon.vic.edu.au

## TERTIARY EDUCATION

### Federation University

Ballarat based university where Nick Shady did his Master's in Business Administration.

www.federation.edu.au

# Bibliography

ABC Rural, (2014). *Succession planning: the good, the bad and the ugly.* [online] Available at: www.abc.net.au/news/2014-07-18/handing-over-the-farm-to-the-next-generation/5602678

Australian Bureau of Statistics - ABS (2014). *4102.0 ABS - Australian Social Trends, Dec 2012.* [online] Available at: www.abs.gov.au/AUSSTATS/abs@.nsf/Lookup/4102.0Main+Features10Dec+2012

AgWeb - Farm Journal Legacy Project. *The Family Meeting.* [online] Available at: www.farmjournallegacyproject.com/the-family-meeting/

AgWeb - Farm Journal Legacy Project. [online] Available at: www.farmjournallegacyproject.com/succession-planning-self-assessment/

AgWeb - Farm Journal Legacy Project. *Legacy Workbook.* [online] Available at: www.farmjournallegacyproject.com/legacy-workbook/

AgWeb - Farm Journal Legacy Project. *Conversation Starters.* [online] Available at: www.farmjournallegacyproject.com/conversation-starters/

Australian Network of Disability (2014). *Disability Statistics.* [online] Available at: www.and.org.au/pages/disability-statistics.html

Australian Institute of Health & Welfare (AIHW) (2014). *Leading types of ill health (AIHW).* [online] Available at: www.aihw.gov.au/australias-health/2014/ill-health

Australian Taxation Office - ATO (2014). *Farm management deposits scheme.* [online] Available at: www.ato.gov.au/Business/Primary-producers/In-detail/Farm-management-deposits-scheme/Farm-management-deposits-scheme/

Australian Taxation Office - ATO (2014). *Farm management deposits scheme.* [online] Available at: www.ato.gov.au/Business/Primary-producers/In-detail/Farm-management-deposits-scheme/Farm-management-deposits-scheme/

Betker, T. (2014). Farm Succession Planning: A Workback Approach. In: *18th International Farm Management Congress.* [online] Available at: www.ifmaonline.org

Covey, S. (1999). *Living the 7 Habits*. New York: Simon & Schuster.

Cropp, R. and Kirkpatrick, J. (2008). *Center for Dairy Profitability.* [online] Pepin County Agriculture Agent. Available at: www.uwex.edu/ ces/farmsuccession/resources/planning/communicationtools/documents/ FarmSucAssessTooldraft7.pdf

Engaging the Y Generation. (2006). [online] Foundations Consulting. Available at: http://www.foundationsconsulting.com.au/docs/EngagingYGeneration.pdf

Farming Ahead (2013). Research Report: Food Security – Safe is better than sorry. April 2013, No. 255. [online] Available at: www.farmingahead.com.au/uploads/ article_item/research-reports/8506/bd68b7c4383caf128ac4a70875684c55.pdf

Farming Ahead (2013). A good project plan can simplify the complex.

[online] Available at: http://multimedia.aspermont.com/download/ FAH_1304_10-11_NEXT_RURAL.pdf

Fleming Muntz Solicitors (2008). Succession and Estate Planning for Country Clients. [online] Available at: www.flemingmuntz.com.au/Publications/ Succession-and-Estate-Planning-for-Country-Clients.aspx

Fryer, D. (2011). *Approaching the Porcupine: Family Farm Business Succession Plan Checklist*. [online] British Columbia Ministry of Agriculture. Available at: www.cattlemen.bc.ca/docs/succession_planning_workshops;_january_2014. pdf

Generations (2014). *BridgeWorks | Generations Keynote Speakers, Experts, Authors, Managing Baby Boomers, Gen Xers and Millennials*. [online] Available at: www.generations.com [

GRDC, Judy Wilkinson & Lyn Sykes (2007). *A Guide to Succession: Sustaining Families and Farms*. [online] Available at: www.grdc.com.au/~/media/1AF010 CCCB374BC1819A63492256EA2E.pdf

Hicks, J., Sappey, R., Basu, P., Keogh, D. and Gupta, R. (2012). *Succession Planning in Australian Farming | Volume 6: Issue 4 Special Issue on Financial Planning*. [online] Australasian Accounting, Business and Finance Journal. Available at: http://ro.uow.edu.au/cgi/viewcontent.cgi?article=1388&context=aabfj

Journal of Extension - JOE (2014). *Later Life Farming: Retirement Plans and Concerns of Farm Families*. [online] Available at: www.joe.org/joe/2010august/a6.php

Lancaster, L. and Stillman, D. (2002). *When generations collide*. New York: HarperCollins.

Meat & Livestock Australia (MLA) (2014). *How prepared are you? Farm business succession planning*. [online] Available at: http://www.mla.com.au/News-and-resources/Industry-news/How-prepared-are-you [Accessed 26 Oct. 2014].

University of Ottawa – Faculty of Medicine (2014). *Generational differences*. [online] Available at: www.med.uottawa.ca/sim/data/Generations_e.htm

North Carolina Farm Transition Network, Inc., (2014). *Farm Succession Planning*. [online] Raleigh. Available at: www.cefs.ncsu.edu/publications/dairy conferenceproceedings/07managingfarmtransitionsbranan.pdf

Ontario Ministry of Agriculture, Food & Rural Affairs (OMAFRA). *Components of a Farm Succession Plan*. [online] Available at: www.omafra. gov.on.ca/english/busdev/facts/10-023.htm

Ontario Ministry of Agriculture, Food & Rural Affairs (OMAFRA). *Farm Succession Planning Steps and Checklist*. [online] Available at: www.omafra. gov.on.ca/english/busdev/facts/10-025.htm

Pioneer (2014). *Pioneer Hi-Bred | Management Advice*. [online] Available at: www.pioneer.com/home/site/us/template.CONTENT/news-commentary/guest-commentary/guid.B7BDCFA7-8706-CD3B-3AE2-0A66D0DCE97D

PNC Bank (2011). *Succession Planning on the Farm*. [online] Available at: www.pnc.com/content/dam/pnc-com/pdf/smallbusiness/IndustrySolutions/Ag_SuccessionPlan_Whitepaper_0111.pdf

National Rural Advisory Council (NRAC) (2012). *Report on the effectiveness of the Farm Management Deposits Scheme*. [online] Available at: www. agriculture.gov.au/SiteCollectionDocuments/ag-food/drought/nrac/fmd-nrac-report.pdf

University of Wollongong (2014). *"Succession Planning in Australian Farming" by John Hicks, Richard Sappey et al..* [online] Available at: http://ro.uow.edu.au/aabfj/vol6/iss4/7

RSM Bird Cameron - Chartered Accountants and Advisory Service, (2014). *Art of planning for succession.* [online] Available at: http://www.rsmi.com.au/Articles-Publications/Art-of-planning-for-succession

Rural Law Online (2005). *Farm Succession Planning: Forum Report.* [online] Available at: www.gwydirshire.com/Council/images/FarmSuccessionPlanningForumReport.pdf

Safe Work Australia, (2014). *Work-related injuries and fatalities on Australian farms - Safe Work Australia.* [online] Available at: www.safeworkaustralia.gov.au/sites/swa/about/publications/pages/work-related-injuries-fatalities-australian-farms

University of Wisconsin - Center for Dairy Profitability, (2014). *5Ds.* [online] Available at: www.cdp.wisc.edu/pdf/5ds.pdf

Weir, G. (2014). *Production Horticulture Farm Succession Planning Toolbox.* [online] Bundaberg Fruit and Vegetable Growers | Australian Vegetable Growers Association. Available at: www.ausveg.com.au/learning-resources/Succession%20Planning.pdf

Wenger, C. for OMAFRA (2014). *Components of a Farm Succession Plan.* OMAFRA Factsheet 04-073. [online] Available at: www.omafra.gov.on.ca/english/busdev/facts/10-023.pdf

www.ingramcontent.com/pod-product-compliance
Lightning Source LLC
Chambersburg PA
CBHW070530200326
41519CB00013B/3004